Price consistency in
development planning

Studies in development and planning Volume 2

Edited by
Centre for Development Planning,
Netherlands School of Economics,
Erasmus University Rotterdam

Editors:
H.C. Bos, P.A. Cornelisse, L.B.M. Mennes
and J.G. Waardenburg

Price consistency in development planning

PETER A. CORNELISSE
Reader in development planning,
Erasmus University,
Rotterdam

Foreword by H.C. Bos,
Professor of development planning,
Erasmus University,
Rotterdam

Rotterdam University Press / 1973

Introduction to the series

This series consists of studies mainly written by staff members of the Centre for Development Planning of the Erasmus University Rotterdam; it represents results of group or individual research. The studies concern subjects which form the field of specialization of the Centre. This field includes, in broad terms, methods and techniques of development planning, analysis of and policies for development, economic policies towards developing countries, as well as the economics of centrally planned systems.

Most of the studies employ a quantitative approach. The common objective of all studies in this series is to contribute, directly or indirectly, to the formulation of policies which aim at furthering the fundamental goals of socio-economic development, at regional, national, multi-national and global levels. The editors express the hope that this broad objective may be reflected in the diversity of contributions to this series.

The editors

Foreword

The economic literature on planning in developing countries has devoted very little systematic attention to the role of prices in formulating development plans. Since the late 'fifties it is recognized that the actual market prices for capital, labour, foreign exchange and often also for commodities do not express the real value of these factors of production and commodities for the economy, and that shadow or accounting prices (Tinbergen) must be used to fulfil this function. It is also well known that in planning models which are formulated as linear programming models dual prices can be derived which measure the scarcity value of the factors or products.

Dr. Cornelisse has made various new contributions to these problems. He distinguishes in his systematic and careful analysis between dual and shadow prices and shows that dual prices can only be used as shadow prices for planning purposes if they are equilibrium prices (price-equilibrium) and if the dual prices can be attained in reality (price-realism). Focussing on the price-equilibrium condition, he shows how equilibrium prices can be derived through an iterative convergent process. This part of the analysis touches on an advanced and abstract chapter in economic theory, the stability of a general competitive system, but the author succeeds in following a pragmatic approach to his subject. This makes his original and illuminating study not only interesting from a theoretical point of view, but also relevant and applicable for practical planning purposes, as the numerical example based on data for the Turkish economy illustrates. I therefore warmly recommend this important study to the attention of those who are concerned in theory or practice with the formulation of development plans.

Henk C. Bos

Preface

In some cases it is hard to decide when a study has reached the stage where it is ready for publication. When I started to work on what I came to call the price-consistency problem, I had only a very vague idea about the direction in which it would lead. There was no working-schedule with a well-defined ultimate objective.

This book contains the account of my experiences when I made an effort to understand this price-consistency problem. It starts with a description of the problem itself and it stops after a discussion of some tentative solution procedures and a simulated application of one of them. So there is a beginning and an end, and there is something in between as there should be. I stopped writing when I felt that there were no wide gaps left in the presentation, in the sense that the usefulness of a further elaboration of one subject did not seem to me to much exceed that of an extension of another subject for better understanding of the present problem.

I realize, of course, that this is a subjective judgment. In any case, the subject matter seems to practically preclude a fully-fledged and well-balanced treatment by one author. For its versatility – which is one of its attractions – presents at the same time a difficulty. Contributions from rather widely different angles have to be taken into consideration, such as welfare economics, market equilibrium, mathematical programming and development planning, to mention only the main fields of study involved. For this reason also I have greatly profited from conversations with other people.

In my acknowledgements I must first mention the Centre for Development Planning of the Erasmus University Rotterdam (formerly of the Netherlands School of Economics) and the Division of Balanced International Growth of the Netherlands Economic Institute, also in Rotterdam. Here I received my formal training in development planning and, during my work there since 1961 (but for two two-year intervals), part of my on-the-job-training as well. The need to think in an orderly fashion was continuously impressed upon me; I have felt this to be a tremendous help every time I could bring myself to applying this lesson. If only for this reason Professors Henk C. Bos and Jan Tinbergen deserve my sincere gratitude.

Everyone doing research knows the stimulating external effects that working together with other research workers can have. On several occasions I have experienced this effect after a casual remark, a suggestion for further reading or a talk with a patiently listening colleague. I gladly take this opportunity to thank my colleagues in Rotterdam for the help they thus gave me.

This study was originally presented as a Ph. D. thesis at the economic faculty of the Erasmus University Rotterdam. Professor Bos, as the supervisor, went through early versions of the manuscript and made a number of suggestions which considerably improved the presentation of the argument. Also Professors C. J. van Eijk and J. Tinbergen provided me with some very useful comments. Jagdish Saigal, my colleague at the Institut Africain de Développement Economique et de Planification in Dakar, Senegal, also has to be mentioned in this connection.

I had a series of very intensive and illuminating discussions with Ad ten Kate which covered nearly the entire manuscript. Thus I benefited enormously in particular from his great knowledge of mathematical programming techniques and, in general, from his original way of thinking. Amongst other things, his remarks directly contributed to my understanding of some crucial matters related with the subject treated in chapter 6. Parts of this chapter are the immediate results of these talks. His contribution is gratefully acknowledged.

Jacob Kol, also of the Centre for Development Planning, did much more than just help me with the computations for the Turkish illustration. During the short period that was available for this exercise, we had very frequent meetings, quite a few of them hilarious to put it mildly, but always with new results and findings. Some of the points made in chapter 7 can be directly traced back to these meetings.

Thanks are also due to the Econometric Institute of the Erasmus University Rotterdam for liberal use of their computer facilities.

Notwithstanding all this excellent help and support, I am afraid that the responsibility for remaining errors and omissions is entirely mine.

It was during my first encounter with the practice of development planning as an OECD-consultant at the State Planning Organization in Ankara, that I became aware of an inconsistency in the traditional planning procedures. In a primitive way, this added to the pleasure I derived from applying the illustrative exercise to Turkey. I am grateful to my friends at s p o who sent me the publications which I needed for that purpose.

The manuscript was typed by Ike Bovenkerk, virtually faultlessly and with remarkable speed. How she managed to do so without neglecting her other tasks still remains a mystery.

It may be a sign of self-conceit to think that my family was deprived of something, whenever, during weekends and evenings, I was working on this book. But if it is not, my wife and children have contributed very much to its completion simply by their quiet acceptation of these frequent periods of physical or mental absence during rather many years.

P. A. Cornelisse

Contents

1. Introduction

1.1. SCOPE OF THE STUDY

The role of prices in techniques of development planning is traditionally only a minor one, even in those cases where the nature of the problem invites an explicit insertion of the price aspect, namely if it involves the operation of demand and supply. This neglect will to some extent be connected with the fact that the market mechanism has been very much out of favour in the theory and practice of development economics since the moment it was realized that the free operation of market forces in underdeveloped countries cannot be relied upon as a guide to a desirable pattern of development.

It is true, of course, that the concept of shadow prices has been formulated precisely for use in development economics. On the other hand however, applications of shadow prices have only been very rare, and then they have often been interpreted erroneously or much too rigidly without the limitations in practical applicability having been taken into account.

The systematic *neglect of the price aspect* in development planning will often lead to a fundamental error in the formulation of development plans. If such a plan goes into some detail distinguishing between different industrial sectors[1], the relative scarcities of products and factors of production implied by it can be interpreted directly as prices. In the vast majority of cases these 'prices' remain dormant and, therefore, unnoticed, although they can come into the open if the programme has been formulated as a linear programming problem. If these 'prices' are different from the prices ruling in reality – which is likely in the underdeveloped

---

1. Let us call this a multi-sector plan corresponding with the middle phase of the planning process (see the next few pages). A multi-sector plan gives the uses and availabilities of the relevant products and productive factors and the levels of magnitude at which economic activities operate, everything in connection with one or more objectives that a country wishes to achieve.

1

world – the programme is rendered *unrealistic*, since its 'price' set does not apply. So, either the actual price set or the 'prices' in the programme must be adjusted, or both, in order that the two sets coincide. If this correction is not made, the programme is incorrect owing to a *price inconsistency*.

This problem, in a nutshell, is the subject of discussion in this book. From its description it can be seen that it really consists of *two sub-problems*: one in which the actual prices (market prices) are adjustable and can be made equal to the programme-prices, and the other in which there is no room for altering the actual prices, which implies that the programme-prices and therefore also the programme itself must be adjusted. This second type of problem is a relatively easy one to solve. However, the first type is pretty complicated and will occupy the greater part of this book.

In the first case, in which the market prices possess a reasonable degree of flexibility, the problem will be to make them coincide with the relative scarcities that the plan involves. As long as this situation is not reached, actual development will deviate from planned development. In other words, there should be equilibrium between the two in terms of prices. Let us call this the *price-equilibrium aspect* of the price-consistency problem.

If, on the other hand, the price of an important factor of production, or commodity can, for some reason, vary only between very narrow bounds, the plan must, of course, take this fact into account. The value it attaches to that item must be in accordance with the realistic price range. This aspect will, therefore, be called the *price-realism aspect* of the price-consistency problem.

Quite clearly, it would be very useful if the 'prices' which may be inherent in a certain development plan helped to achieve optimal efficiency of the economy to which the plan refers. If they possessed this property they would be an ideal guideline for the orientation of a price policy concurrent with the development policy. By definition, shadow prices have precisely these characteristics, so our discussion will profit a great deal from earlier contributions which have already treated and elaborated on this concept. On the other hand, it should be made clear, even at this early stage, that indiscriminate application of shadow prices will not be advocated here.

The position adopted in this book is that, even if market forces are not reliable indicators for economic development, they nevertheless exist. Demand exists and supply exists, and both react to a greater or lesser degree to price variations. A development plan does not improve, if these factors are simply ignored, whereas, on the other hand, its operational power is likely to increase if it takes into account these factors satisfactorily. Briefly, if a development programme involves – perhaps only implicitly – a considerable price variation, namely if the prices inherent in the programme deviate significantly from the actual prices, the relevant market forces are to be included in the analysis, whereas price restrictions must be introduced in those cases when an actual price change is not feasible. A consistent approach which could cope with these complications would help to avoid unrealistic decisions and the economic tensions they create, and to enhance the quality and success of development plans.

By its very nature, the need to take account of the price element is strongest for the type of operations corresponding with – in TINBERGEN's terminology – the middle phase of the planning-in-stages procedure[2]. This procedure is concerned with the quantitative aspects of a development plan. It differentiates three main stages: the *macrophase*, which deals with the most desirable development in macro-economic terms; the *middle phase*, in which the economy is subdivided in industrial sectors and regions; and the *microphase*, which deals with separate projects and smaller geographical units. Naturally, the breakdown of an economy into sectors of production calls for a procedure by which supply of and demand for the finished and semi-finished products of these sectors are matched. The two main approaches which can be used for this purpose are the commodity-balance procedure and the input-output method. However, if demand and supply by sectors (products) are to meet in the middle phase, the prices under which the balance can be reached deserve special attention. Particularly so, since it is even unlikely that a multisector plan will end up in an equilibrium situation, if it is not explicitly taken care of.

At this stage the relative sophistication of the techniques and data required to establish a price-consistent development plan will certainly limit the *applicability* of the corrective procedures. Few countries are equipped with the statistical and planning apparatus that would meet these requirements. Consequently, the direct operational value of what follows here is equally restricted. Of course, the same can be said of, for example, the input-output analysis. Even though this concept is widely known nowadays, a large number of countries is still not in a position to apply it in practice. The value of the concept for these countries lies in the fact that it has solidly implanted among policy makers the awareness of the strong interdependencies between productive activities. Similarly,

2. J. TINBERGEN, 1967, chapters 6, 7, 8 and 9.

3

in the immediate future the contribution of the price-consistency concept for many countries will probably merely be the realization that, first, the scarcities implied by a development programme are not necessarily in accordance with the scarcity ratios reflected by the actual prices, and that, second, a wide disparity may endanger the outcome of the programme. This book may be helpful in propagating this realization. At the same time, the discussion may help the reader to form an opinion on the effectiveness of the available theoretical framework to deal with the price-consistency problem.

It has been advocated that, whenever relevant, a book should indicate which parts contain an original contribution. Although this practice brings with it the danger for the author that his claims to originality will appear to be immodest or even unjust, readers who wish to concentrate on these parts will appreciate a brief indication of their contents and where to find them.

The idea to write this book came to me when I was helping to formulate a linear programming model for the Turkish economy at the Turkish State Planning Organization, Ankara. We had to find out whether such a model could assist in identifying the industrial sectors which would be suitable for import substitution and/or export promotion. It occurred to me then how illogical it would be to base estimates of possible future export earnings on the official exchange rate of the seriously overvalued Turkish lira, when the solution to the model could be expected to come up with a different exchange rate. Knowing that the official rate was 'wrong', one might even be tempted to require of a 'correct' model that it would produce a *different* exchange rate. I suppose that other planners have had similar experience[3], but, as far as I know, this book contains the first systematic treatment of this price-consistency problem, even if it uses concepts and procedures which have already been known for some time. Thus, the next chapters explain the *relevance of price consistency* in the theory and practice of development planning, the *type of error* which is made if it is ignored, and the *effects* that this will have on the outcome of the plan. *Procedures* which can help to solve the problem are examined together with the statistical requirements.

In a more specific sense, new elements can also be found in what will be called here the excess-price approach (sections 5.3., 5.4. and 6.5.). The programming algorithm which is based on the excess-price adaptations

3. In fact, when I talked about it with M. BRUNO of the Bank of Israel, in Ankara in 1966, he told me he had already come to the same conclusion. The essence of the price-consistency concept emerges also in MYRDAL's critical appraisal of accounting prices (G. MYRDAL, 1968, appendix 5). See also section 3.4.

has been presented in section 6.5., but the underlying arguments come up for discussion in earlier chapters. Further, special attention has been given to the link between stability conditions for general equilibrium and conditions for convergence of programming problems which incorporate general equilibrium.

1.2. OUTLINE OF THE CONTENTS

The book can be divided into three parts. The *first part* introduces the price-consistency problem by discussing the relevant aspects of prices in developing countries and development planning.

The 'language' of the *second part* is different, as frequent use is made of mathematical formulations. It deals with the case when actual prices have some freedom of movement so that they can be readjusted, if there is good reason to believe that a different price level corresponds better with a desired pattern of development. It will be argued subsequently that such ideal prices also have to be equilibrium prices, a subject that has a mathematical tradition since WALRAS. Experience with mathematical economics has shown that a very real danger exists that mathematical interpretations of economic reality start to live a life of their own, rather than simply remaining the technical instrument – with limited possibilities – that they really are. On the other hand, the virtues of this approach in terms of efficiency and the insight often gained by it have already been demonstrated, but one great disadvantage of the use of mathematics in this case is that this language is not commonly known among development planners. Nevertheless, this part requires a basic knowledge of differential calculus, matrix algebra and linear programming. The first part of the book is meant to compensate for this although it cannot do so entirely.

Finally, the *third part* contains an illustrative exercise, intended to give an idea of the computational characteristics of an actual treatment of the price-consistency problem. It was meant, more especially, to specify and examine some complications in a simulated application of a procedure devised to deal with that problem.

A rather large number of the concepts and procedures employed in this book are not commonly used among planners. It would probably have been convenient for the reader if most of them had been introduced in it too, in order that references be directly at hand. Unfortunately, this approach would have inflated the book so enormously that it proved to be impractical. An effort has been made, however, to include references to the relevant literature whenever a new subject likely to be unfamiliar to interested planners is discussed.

Chapter 2 concentrates on the price-equilibrium aspect. It discusses the *main characteristics* of the *price systems* in developing countries and their shortcomings as pathfinders for optimum resource allocation. This leads directly to a discussion of the ideal counterpart, namely shadow pricing. I shall first indicate why a licensing system designed to maintain incorrect official prices may lead involuntarily to a set of effective prices that approach the shadow prices. Hence, under these circumstances actual resource allocation may not be as bad as one might expect if one concentrates on the performance of official prices as scarcity indicators. The equilibrating quality that shadow prices must possess is also discussed in this chapter.

Chapter 3 is concerned with the price-realism aspect and describes some ways in which an optimal *price policy* can be *implemented*. A number of serious, practical limitations to such a policy will prove to exist in the developing world. In particular the prices of some key-factors are subject to such great restrictions, limiting severely the range of values they can adopt, that trespassing into territory beyond them would render a policy unrealistic. This will have to be taken into account in a development programme.

The next chapter attempts to indicate the extent to which inclusion of the price-consistency concept in the formulation of a development plan affects the *preparatory work* and the *outcome*. The additional statistical information required is examined and we shall see that the existence of price restrictions will help to reduce the statistical requirements which would otherwise be impossibly burdensome. A speculative comparison of the outcome of a multi-sector plan with and without the price-consistency concept has also been included. Chapter 4 – and the first part of the book – concludes with a summary scheme which brings together the main concepts and their interrelations, the problems they entail and their consequences as they have been discussed in the text.

In chapter 5 the second part of the book starts with a discussion of various types of *equilibrium* and the relation between optimum and equilibrium. An illustrative example is presented and analysed rather extensively in order to demonstrate, in the simplest possible way, the operation and effect of a number of procedures and factors related to the solution of the price-equilibrium problem. An iterative procedure has been followed to simulate the path of a fictitious enterpreneur's adaptation in search of a price set and a production programme reflecting a situation of equilibrium and satisfying a simple optimality criterion. Thereafter the stability conditions of a price equilibrium are derived and discussed on the basis of two different adaptation patterns. Larger and larger market systems are examined, culminating in the type of set-up that appears frequently in multi-sector planning, where a distinction is made between different products (sectors), their interdependencies according to the input-output matrix, different factors of production, demand for which depends linearly on the volumes of sectoral production. But here, contrary the development planning procedure, prices of products and factors and their effect on demand for the former and supply of the latter have been taken into account explicitly. In this chapter also the degree of realism of the assumptions that have to be made in order to arrive at conclusions, will be critically examined.

After the discussion of the concept of equilibrium in chapter 5, chapter 6 goes on to incorporate a criterion for optimization as well, so mathematical programming procedures make their appearance. First the concepts of Lagrangian function and saddle point are briefly introduced, whereafter the uncommon structure is explained of the '*equilibrium programming problem*' which emerges when the price-consistency aspect is included in a programming problem.

The various techniques for solving this problem are discussed in widely differing degrees of detail. For didactical reasons only those procedures which resemble closely the iterative methods in equilibrium problems inspired by the adaptive behaviour patterns, discussed in chapter 5, have been treated at some length. Other algorithms have been indicated only very briefly for the sake of completeness at the end of the chapter. The reason for this discrimination is that this book has been written in the first place to describe the nature and implications of the price-consistency concept in development planning. The actual solution of the technical problems it involves is, however, the work of a very small group of highly specialized econometricians and mathematicians. Even though the use of mathematics was felt to be unavoidable in this chapter, a discussion of these other solution techniques has therefore been left aside.

The algorithm originating from a familiar adaptation procedure in equilibrium theory, discussed here in detail, is the one presented by CHENERY, KRETSCHMER and UZAWA. Also in the examination of its mathematical background, the link with the concepts of the general equilibrium (one of our main preoccupations) has been demonstrated and emphasized on several occasions. Other algorithms based on different adaptation patterns are conceivable and one – the excess-price algorithm – is extensively discussed and compared with the first. Finally, some concluding remarks include a brief indication of alternative solution procedures.

The illustrative exercise for Turkey presented in chapter 7 does not pretend to possess any normative value. It provides an opportunity, however, to investigate some practical complications in a correction procedure towards price consistency. This simulation will demonstrate, for example, that the multi-sector model with which this problem is to be tackled, requires great attention. For, without provision for the rigidities inherent in such a model, it will be inappropriate for that purpose. Also it proves necessary to see to it that all value magnitudes remain expressed in constant prices, even if variable prices are explicitly allowed for in the evaluation of the parameters. Finally, though inconclusive as an illustration necessarily is, and taking into account the limited scope of the exercise, it appears that the error made if price consistency is ignored can indeed be considerable.

2. Prices in developing countries

2.1. MARKET PRICES

2.1.1. Economic reality versus theoretical optimum

Ideally, prices should reflect underlying scarcities in such a way that an optimal allocation of resources occurs if they are applied in taking economic decisions. In other words, all resources would have to be employed in combinations that correspond inversely with their relative scarcities, in such a way that a certain welfare indicator cannot be increased by changing these combinations. This matter is within the province of the theory of *welfare economics* which specifies the conditions to be satisfied to achieve the optimum. Reality, however, proves to compare very crudely with these specifications. Or, if we reverse this conclusion: the theory of welfare economics loses touch with reality when an existing adverse situation cannot be changed to render some of its conclusions non-applicable in practical exercises. Still, the theory may be a useful device in identifying the markets operating grossly out of tune, which in turn facilitates a better approximation to the optimal situation if proper measures can be taken.

Various deviations stand in the way of the theoretical optimum, such as the absence of perfect competition at one or both sides of a large number of markets, other than economic reasons influencing market decisions, direct intervention in the price mechanism, taxes and insufficient response to changing circumstances. All these factors *disrupt* the direct link between prices and underlying scarcities. Occasionally, supply and demand may not even match at the prevailing market prices, and often the distortion is then directly apparent.

However, one must not imagine that the disturbing factors, as far as they can be avoided, have only a disadvantageous effect. For example, a market may have become monopolistic or oligopolistic because economies of scale enabled the large firms to compete smaller ones out of

9

the market. The result may well be that products can now be offered at a lower price because operating costs will have dropped. This situation would not be improved if perfect competition were forcefully restored by dividing the supply side of the market among a large number of production units. Of course, this is different from saying that a deviation from the perfectly competitive market is therefore in the interest of the community. The example is meant to illustrate that a deviation may be perfectly acceptable if the adverse effects – *i.e.* the inequality between prices and marginal costs – do not take serious proportions.

It is not my intention in this chapter to go into a detailed analysis of the optimality conditions and the aspects of deviations in the blueprint of the theoretical optimum from economic reality. The interested reader is referred to T. SCITOVSKY, 1951 and I. M. D. LITTLE, 1963. However, we are not entirely relieved of the need to discuss a few points at some more length because of the special position taken by developing countries. The reason is that, though price disturbances occur in industrialized and developing countries alike, they appear to do so in *different degrees*. The nature and causes of the prominence of these deviations in the developing world have already been investigated elsewhere[1], but it will be useful to comment upon them in the rest of this section as an introduction to our discussion of the action that can be taken to achieve a more efficient resource allocation. As their inappropriateness as scarcity indicators reaches often alarming proportions and also because their impact is large and wide-spread, special attention will be devoted to the wage rate, the rate of interest and the rate of exchange.

It is in the nature of less developed economies that the tendency towards an equilibrium with an optimal resource allocation is very slight. A low level of economic activity, social and bureaucratic inflexibility, intervention as a policy instrument, poor communications and shortage of entrepreneurial skills are common features in developing countries which help to create and maintain the price disturbances referred to above. Similar phenomena, or others with the same effect, are at work in industrialized countries, but only on a smaller scale.

Further, it must not be forgotten that the optimality conditions are derived with a view to economic welfare exclusively, which is of course only a part of any *general* welfare optimum. The social injustices that would result under an *economic* optimum may reach giant proportions especially in developing countries and require measures that necessarily

1. For references, see H. B. CHENERY, 1959.

turn from this optimum. A part of intervention does, in fact, originate from this necessity.

Taxes stand out separately in the list of disturbing factors. As regards the other factors, an attempt may be made to improve the situation directly by removing their causes. As a society without taxes is inconceivable, and with the role of the government growing in many market economies, one can only attempt to reduce the disturbing effects that taxes may have in relation to the optimal distribution of resources. Rather ironically, taxes are also proposed as an important means of achieving better functioning of an economy (see section 3.2.).

2.1.2. Factor prices in underdeveloped economies

Let us first briefly investigate the *labour market* in a prototype developing country with its vast excess supply of unskilled labour and of some types of skilled labour, so as to find out how and why it settles at a sub-optimal position. In economies where unskilled labour is abundantly available, wages will naturally be under a strong downward pressure. There is even no economic reason why they would not drop to zero if the pressure were strong enough, *i.e.* if excess labour supply is still hanging over the market at a positive wage. In reality, however, wages meet strong resistance from below which refrains them from falling below a certain level despite the permanent existence of the downward pressure.

The *counterpressure* comes from the interaction of a number of factors in the social and sociological sphere[2]. Part of the explanation derives from the requirement that a person and his nearest dependants must be able to survive on the wage earned. Society would not accept an employer who offered less; but even if that were so, no employee can accept a wage on which he could not make a living. In fact, he can often indeed afford to decline a too low wage offer, if he is protected by the rules of the extended family system under which those who are without income are supported by better-off relatives. For similar reasons, under self-employment, the price which sellers must ask for their products or services cannot drop below a minimum level. These forces, sometimes strengthened legislatively, are strong enough to maintain the wage rate at a subsistence level, which allows a living even if it is miserable and, on the average, of short duration.

---

2. For a more extensive discussion, see for example, P.T. BAUER and B.S. YAMEY, 1963, p. 76 *et seq.*

11

The *subsistence-wage level* is not an absolute datum. In fact, it may vary rather widely, not so much with the relative size of the unemployed manpower population, but rather with the level of material well-being of the nation as a whole. For the present short examination, it is enough, however, to observe that the condition of social acceptability of the wage rate builds a floor in the labour market below which the wage rate will not operate. Although this seems a good thing, the problem is not really solved by it.

The minimum wage makes labour more expensive than it would be without it and consequently limits demand. Massive unemployment is often the result, causing hardship to those who are the victim of it, and a loss to the economy as a whole, since a part of the labour supply is cut off from production. Apparently, therefore, the ruling market forces do not lead to an optimal allocation of labour.

Above we mentioned that laws may help to prevent proper functioning (from the purely economic point of view) of the price mechanism. This is not confined to the price of labour only, but can, amongst other things, be extended to commodities, as is notoriously the case with agricultural commodities. Here again the aim is to guarantee a *minimum income*, in this case to farmers. As they are often self-employed, the most common and efficient procedure is to fix minimum prices for their agricultural products. This phenomenon is also well known, but unlike the wage disequilibrium, can be observed in both developed and developing countries. The effect is similar though: agricultural products tend to be overpriced and, therefore, in excess supply. Once more, the relief provided does not remove the basic problem.

Intervention in the price mechanism may also be due to other than social considerations, namely if prices are applied as an instrument of economic policy. Thus we see that in order to stimulate industrialization governments in some developing countries keep the *interest rate* artificially low. The assumption is that industrialization will take place at a slower pace if the price of capital is left free to the influences of the normal conditions prevailing on the capital market.

Naturally, the excess demand for capital that is the result of the intervention must be controlled, because otherwise the fixed rate of interest cannot be maintained. This leads to a policy of capital *rationing*, in which the state rather than the market decides how the available capital supply will be distributed among enterprises[3]. Remarkably

3. A similar procedure can be set up in order to curb agricultural overproduction. Only in this case the state would have to restrict supply, for example by regulating the size of the cultivated area.

enough, if the state were to act precisely as the market would have done, the only difference would be that now enterprises make a larger profit, as they pay less interest for the capital they employ. This extra profit may indeed stimulate industrialization, not only because higher profits make it more attractive to set up a business, but also because larger amounts can be ploughed back for expansion purposes (the reinvestment argument).

However, the interest rate may also be kept down in order to prevent the 'unearned income' (income without labour effort, but not income transfers) from becoming unduly high. The motive in this case is of a social, political or ethical nature.

Another well-known example of a pre-fixed price is the *rate of exchange*. Developing countries import the great majority of their investment goods (excluding the construction component) from abroad. So in order to speed up the accumulation of capital goods, and thus to promote an increase in production, especially in the industrial sectors, many developing countries maintain a rate of exchange that undervalues foreign currency. By doing so, the importation of machinery and equipment and also of other goods is made very attractive. Once again, the continuous upward pressure on imports that is the result may well lead to an undesirably large deficit on the balance of payments which forces the policy makers to adopt additional measures. One way to deal with this problem is to establish a system of import *licences* in which priority is given to commodities directly required for production expansion. Another way is to create a system of multiple exchange rates with increasingly unfavourable rates the closer the commodity approaches the luxury, nonnecessity category. Still another policy could consist of applying different rates of import duties and taxes to different classes of commodities. In most cases the import policy is a combination of these three approaches.

Next to such a policy measure fixing the price of foreign currency, there may be other factors at work such as the movement of the terms of trade against developing countries[4]. With international prices for their export products sagging in a market in which demand is growing only slowly and price elasticities are generally low, devaluation may not help

4. In fact, for the developing world *as a whole*, the evidence is not entirely conclusive, but since the downward trend is generally believed to have persisted for two decades now, with exceptions only due to acute international crises, it is an illustration of the difficulties that developing countries have in adapting themselves to changing circumstances. In this case capital shortage, lack of technologies adapted to their resource endowments and of entrepreneurial skill and the protective trade policies of the industrialized countries are mainly responsible for the inertia.

to increase export earnings directly. But, since a structural improvement of export performances can only come from the introduction of new products, devaluation may render exportation of these products profitable after some time.

An overvalued currency under a fixed exchange rate may also be the result of an excessive rate of inflation as compared with the rest of the world and especially the main trading partners. An adaptation of the price of foreign exchange is then often felt to be an admission of the failure of domestic economic policy. Also other more abstract feelings of national pride surrounding the rate of exchange stand a devaluation in the way before the situation has become untenable. G. C. WINSTON, 1970, draws attention to another category with a vested interest in official overvaluation of domestic currency, consisting of those who practise overinvoicing applications for foreign exchange. The extra amount obtained in this way can be sold at an open market price and, thus, the profit made on this type of operation is a function of the extent of the official undervaluation of foreign exchange. Estimates of the amounts of profits involved are obviously very shaky, but under certain circumstances they can be considerable, and so can be the pressure from this side to maintain the situation, while using, of course, different arguments.

Whatever the motives are, official exchange rates do differ – sometimes widely – from the true price of foreign currency, especially in developing countries[5]. It implies firstly that supply and demand differ from each other and, secondly, that an optimal allocation cannot be obtained with the prevailing price mechanism.

Our discussion of the adverse effects of intervention in the price mechanism must not, we emphasize, suggest that the *laissez-faire* type of free-market economy is defended here as the system leading to optimal allocation of resources. On the contrary, the circumstances in developing countries are such that a free-market economy is quite clearly sub-optimal mainly due to poor communications, the absence of information about production and sales possibilities, an embryonic capital market, an inadequate education system, lack of organizational and entrepreneurial skill, and so on. Further, in as far as state intervention is not already justified for other than economic reasons, its positive effects (for example on industrialization) may possibly outweigh its negative effects. This discussion was only meant to show that the market mechanism *cannot be ignored*, even if it is considered as an unreliable guide towards economic

---

5. A. O. KRUEGER, 1966, among others, in an interesting exercise has made an attempt to estimate the effects of undervalued foreign exchange for the Turkish economy.

development. An evaluation of state intervention may, in fact, point in the opposite direction, as it can be argued that, given the inevitable circumstances leading away from the theoretical optimum, a public authority should be empowered to act to reduce the misallocation to the minimum[6].

However, the conclusion that we are aiming at is that policy makers cannot easily introduce price intervention in view of one specific desired effect and ignore all the other consequences. When evaluating the pros and cons of such an intervention, the entire result must of course be considered, and it may well be that the adverse effects which would otherwise occur, require an alternative measure or additional measures. The essence of the argument is that the effects of intervention in the price mechanism appear to reach much farther than is often realized.

In other words, there is a need for an improvement of the practice of evaluating the effects of intervention in the price mechanism. This book is closely connected with that problem, for it is concerned with the examination of the theoretical framework that can be used to find a price structure which corresponds with the aims and constraints of a socio-economic development plan. One thing is clear already: if market prices lead to misallocations, apparently a separate set of prices will have to be derived which do not possess this shortcoming and which must, therefore, be *independent* of these market prices.

2.2. EFFICIENT RESOURCE ALLOCATION

2.2.1. Introduction

Market prices may fail, therefore, on two counts: they may not equate demand and supply and/or they may fail to steer anywhere near an efficient resource allocation. It will be necessary to discuss some aspects of the latter subject, if only very briefly.

According to SCITOVSKY's well-known definition, an *efficient resource allocation* is one that corresponds with the *community's preference*[7], implying that the one depends on the other. In other words, a difference of opinion may exist as to how resources should be allocated optimally, as the community's preference may be evaluated differently by different

6. For example, O. LANGE, in O. LANGE and F. M. TAYLOR, 1938, p. 107, on these market imperfections: 'This adds a (...) powerful argument to the economist's case for socialism'.
7. *Ibid.*

15

persons. Consequently, a difference of opinion regarding a desirable allocation does not necessarily mean that the underlying theory is wrong, or that the theory is erroneously interpreted or misunderstood, as seems to be thought very often. On the one hand, it requires a precise description of what the community's preference is supposed to mean. Very often planners assume that it can be represented by the preference function of the *state*. This solution seems to be the simplest way out of the dilemma of how to express the multitude of interdependent individual preferences. The state's preference function is then viewed as an approximation of the resultant of the individuals' preferences. This function may even obtain an additional quality if it is agreed that the 'short-sightedness' of individuals' preferences can be avoided by the state. If indeed the state 'knows better', its preference function will be preferable to the agglomerate function when it comes to an efficient allocation of resources.

It will hardly be necessary to add that one assumes here that the state will only act in the interest of the people it serves. Otherwise, the dangers of 'big-brotherism' are obvious. Again there may be grave differences of opinion as to what is in 'the true interest of the people', which may raise questions of moral integrity among those carrying out the policy of the state, even if it is accepted that the latter is of good will.

Still another question is sometimes raised. We have observed already that the theory of welfare economics lacks direct practical applicability, so one may argue, as LITTLE[8] does, that there is no theoretical warrant that a change in the direction of the theoretical optimum will be good or desirable. Nevertheless, he agrees that the national income could be increased by such a change, namely if the price system is greatly out of line with the optimality conditions derived in that theory. It may be added that when he formulated this cautious view, LITTLE apparently projected the theory upon the situation in an average industrialized country, where, as we have argued, structural disequilibria tend to be much less prominent than in the developing world. Therefore, it seems reasonable to assume that an appropriate measure in line with the welfare economics theory will indeed improve the situation, especially in a developing country.

The foregoing section discussed some structural market disequilibria in developing countries. Without going into the many optimality conditions themselves, we will now examine briefly and schematically why this may have a detrimental effect on an efficient resource allocation. Again we concentrate on the prices of primary factors.

8. *Ibid.*

Let us first take the wage rate. Since they cannot drop below the subsistence level and for other reasons, wages are clearly not perfectly flexible. It may be – and in most developing countries this holds true – that the subsistence wage does not clear the market, in the sense that individuals offer their services without finding employment. In technical terms this situation is one in which the marginal rate of substitution between work and leisure is not equal for all individuals. More concretely, it means that productive services available at the market wage remain unused. Such services would have increased total production, only the value of the increase would have been smaller than the wage costs involved in it. From the employer's point of view, the decision to employ no more *labour* is, therefore, perfectly rational.

This is different for society as a whole, because people, if employed, add to production, whereas employed or unemployed, they must be supported anyway. It follows that, from society's point of view, additional labour should be employed until its marginal product has dropped to zero[9], because the allocation of additional labour will add to physical production, with the result that national income at constant prices will increase with it. Even at this point there may be surplus labour, but at least better use has now been made of the available labour stock. On the other hand, there is also the possibility that the labour supply is exhausted when the marginal productivity is still positive, so that the optimum allows a full employment of labour.

Contrary to the case of labour, the costs of *capital* in developing countries tend to underestimate its scarcity, and capital will be disposed of too easily[10]. This may be reflected in the selection of production techniques with a high capital intensity if less capital-intensive techniques are available, or in the production of commodities that require relatively much capital. With a higher price of capital such ventures would have become less profitable or might even have incurred losses and would not have been executed. Relatively more capital would thus have become available for capital-extensive projects which yield a higher rate of return per unit of capital. A higher level of production and employment could therefore be obtained with the same capital stock, if capital-intensive projects could no longer compete successfully at the capital market.

Finally, the rate of exchange is often kept constant even if the balance of payments is apparently in disequilibrium. As far as demand for

---

9. The usual assumption has been made that, with other factors constant, the marginal productivity of labour falls as employment increases.
10. W. F. STOLPER, 1966, p. 193 *et seq.* presents an analysis of a proper interest policy.

foreign currency is concerned, the effects will be much the same as those described for underpriced capital, so they will not be repeated here. There is one important difference, however, on the supply side.

Whereas the supply of capital is highly price inelastic, hardly reacting to significant changes in the rate of interest, the supply of foreign currency, as a result of changes in the volume of exports, may be expected to vary with the rate of exchange. Undervaluation of foreign currency will thus have a two-sided effect. Assuming that world market prices will remain unaffected, a devaluation will bring about a reduction of demand for foreign currency in the absence of adverse price reactions, whereas supply will increase as marginal projects become internationally competitive. The equilibrating mechanism may thus operate from both sides.

2.2.2. *Optimal allocation and substitution possibilities*

At this point a remark must be added on the possibility of *choosing* between ventures of *different factor intensities* in reality. Availability of such a choice is a necessary condition in the above train of thought. For a short examination of this matter it will be helpful, first to distinguish between *national* and *international sectors*, as TINBERGEN[11] does. According to his definition, national sectors are those which produce commodities that cannot cross national borders for political or technical reasons. Examples are construction, education, government administration etc. Together they are estimated to contribute approximately thirty to forty per cent of national income. The other sectors produce commodities that can be traded internationally and are, therefore, called international sectors.

Only products from international sectors (international products) offer a choice between *domestic production* and *imports*. Products that can compete with foreign goods will be produced at home and may be exported, whereas the others will be obtained from abroad. In this post-Leontief-paradox era it may be added that under proper factor prices and in the absence of too many trade restrictions, international trade thus offers the opportunity to economize on scarce factors of production. This possibility is, by definition, not available for national products, where only the *production techniques* can be adapted to the prevailing conditions. Unfortunately however, the variation in incremental capital-output ratios proves, for instance, to be especially large among national sectors, whereas the range of ratios between international sectors tends

11. J. TINBERGEN, 1965.

18

to be fairly small, as MENNES, TINBERGEN and WAARDENBURG[12] have shown with Indian data.

One may wonder, of course, if the examination of one particular country supplies sufficient evidence to warrant a conclusion, because India, being a capital-poor country, will have concentrated on those international products that require relatively little capital. Such a tendency would clearly limit the range of capital intensities for international products in India to the low values. However, the above conclusion would still seem to apply, because an international comparison of capital coefficients of international products[13] suggests that, though they are higher in industrialized countries, they do not vary as widely as capital coefficients of national sectors in individual countries. A subsequent study by the Netherlands Economic Institute, Rotterdam, on labour intensities came to a similar conclusion. We must therefore conclude that the existing possibilities of factor substitution through the *international division of labour* obviously remain rather limited and the more so, if the restrictive trade policies pursued by the industrialized nations are also taken into consideration.

This conclusion is further aggravated by the fact that the range of choice between *production techniques* of different factor intensities is also rather limited. The reason is that present-day production processes originate predominantly in the industrialized part of the world. Consequently they bear the marks of the scarcity conditions prevailing there, viz. relative capital abundance and labour scarcity. Techniques developed there are designed for large scale production and will tend to be labour-saving, and technological progress will intensify this trend still further. Although precisely these qualities render the production techniques unfit for developing countries, factory lay-out and type of machinery are often the same as in industrialized nations, for lack of modern alternatives. So, unless something is done about these rigidities, the possibilities of a better adaptation of the productive process to the proportions of available prime factors in developing countries will be seriously impaired.

Hence, it would be a great step forward if countries with surplus labour would stimulate practical research for and the application of labour-intensive techniques of production. But, apart from countries like China, Taiwan, North and South Korea and, in a way, Japan, this is hardly the case. With a view to the pressing need for a better allocation of resources – and coupled with this, the necessity to improve the disas-

12. L. B. M. MENNES, J. TINBERGEN and J. G. WAARDENBURG, 1969, p. 268.
13. E. J. SCHREUEL, 1970, Table 4.

trous employment situation in many less developed countries – one must conclude that action in this field deserves a very high priority, very much higher than it has had until now. (For a survey of this subject and an indication of measures that can be taken to this end, see K. MARSDEN, 1970.)

2.3. SHADOW PRICES

Shadow prices – or true prices, accounting prices, objectively-determined prices or correct prices as they are sometimes also called – are typically the prices that guide towards a more efficient allocation of scarce resources. The farther the actual market prices deviate from them, the more they are needed. Section 2.1. already mentioned that under a licence system, a public institution rather than the market will have to decide on the distribution of the available resources. If this institution had a set of shadow prices at hand, it could carry out its task in the best possibly way. For example, if the market rate of interest underrates the scarcity of capital, it should issue capital only to those enterprises that would not operate at a loss even if the shadow rate of interest were applied. This shadow rate would have been fixed at such a level that demand for capital at that price just exhausts supply.

This example illustrates the case of an upward adjustment of the market price. The case of a downward adjustment may be somewhat different, owing to the fact that a price cannot drop below zero. Suppose that even at a wage of zero, demand for labour is still smaller than the total manpower stock[14], so that unemployment will continue to prevail. Under these circumstances even the shadow price would evidently not be able to clear the market. It occurs, as was indicated above, if additionally employed labour does not add to production; a situation which may conceivably materialize in a barren country with an extremely small stock of capital. Even production techniques with a very high labour intensity might then leave a part of the working-age population unemployed.

Until now, we have mainly considered situations in which only one shadow price had to be handled. In reality, of course, *several* shadow prices of factors and products may simultaneously deviate significantly

14. The term 'total manpower stock' is preferred here to 'supply of labour', as the latter would suggest that labour would still be supplied at sub-subsistence-wage levels. As we have already argued that income from labour cannot drop below a certain minimum subsistence level, an inconsistency would otherwise have occurred. This matter will be further dealt with in the next chapter.

from actual prices. This makes the situation only slightly more complicated, for as soon as the shadow prices have been determined, they can be applied for the same type of test as was described above. Applications which have passed the test should be granted the necessary volumes of all the prime factors and goods required.

The discussion of shadow prices in the literature relates mostly to factors of production rather than to commodities, though their prices may equally possess certain deficiencies. The explanation can probably be found in the same arguments with which our preoccupation with prime factors was justified above: actual prices of factors of production tend to be farther out of focus than those of commodities, whereas, in addition, the effect of false pricing of the former is felt throughout the economy as cost components and as sources of income. For purposes of illustration, reference to factors of production is, therefore, more striking. It should not be forgotten, however, that actual prices of commodities may also need adjustment.

2.4. THE COSTS OF PERSUASION

It can be argued that under a system which controls the use of factors and products in excess demand by issuing licences, the *nominal costs* as indicated by the market prices officially charged are not a fair representation of the *actual costs* incurred by the users. For, in order to obtain a licence, an additional effort must be made, which would not have been needed if the product or factor concerned could have been obtained at an open market. First, an application must be made describing for what purpose the requested amounts are to be used, together with a detailed statement of the costs and revenues involved. It will take time and skill to prepare such an application. A decision cannot be expected right away, because the organization issuing the licences will have to check whether the information supplied with the application is indeed correct. Only when this has been verified can it be decided whether or not the request deserves to be met. Meanwhile the applicant may have been called in for further clarification, or he may have volunteered to do so in order to add to his arguments or he may have spent some money in order to lubricate the decision-making process.

The procedure of *persuasion* as it is roughly sketched here will probably have missed a few stages, but even then it takes time, effort and skill, which all add to the costs of obtaining licenced goods. It means that, as was said at the beginning of this section, the nominal market prices underestimate the actual costs. Only those who can afford to pay the additional costs, that is those who attach a higher value to the good than is indicated by the official price, will be prepared to go through the process of obtaining a licence. Sometimes the extra costs are institutionalized when licences are sold to the highest bidder. It will be clear that the stimulating effect on industrialization will now have been completely lost. It can only be defended as a device to increase public revenue.

All this amounts to the conclusion that, if a price is fixed at a level which underestimates the scarcity of the good or factor concerned so that a system of licences has to maintain the price, the system itself will tend to raise the costs for the users of the item. As in such a case the shadow price would be higher than the market price, this means that this system redresses unintentionally the deficiencies of the market price it supports. In fact, if the costs of persuasion are so high that the licencing authority does not have to turn down even one application, if supply is just exhausted and assuming that discrimination between applicants does not exist, there would be no difference with the ideal open market situation as far as the allocation of resources is concerned. In such a situation the industrialization incentive is no longer effective; there would only be the loss incurred by the costs of operating a useless licence organization. Evidently, such a hypothetical situation is not likely to materialize. Still, though it is an extreme case, it illustrates that, in the end, the undervaluation of a scarce factor as an incentive may be less effective than is sometimes thought.

2.5. THE DERIVATION OF SHADOW PRICES

The use of shadow prices makes sense only when they differ from the market prices observed in reality. As shadow prices are not employed in actual transactions, they can only be determined in a rather abstract way. A decision to determine an alternative set of shadow prices can only be based on an impression that a difference will exist. Hence, it becomes necessary to look out for signs indicating that the actual prices do not function properly. These indications have been outlined briefly in section 2.1. Generally the signs can easily be observed. The real difficulties arise when it comes to *assessing the value of the shadow prices*.

Since the possibility of direct measurement in the real world does not exist, shadow prices have to be determined on the basis of a *simulated reality*, where disturbances that stand in the way of the optimum, are not allowed to exist. In other words, a model will have to be built describing the working of the market forces, their interactions and the other factors with which interdependencies exist. More specifically, it should include the relationships between volumes of supply and demand on the one hand and the corresponding prices on the other, substitution possibilities between and complementarities of different factors or products, production functions and consumption and investment functions, etc. The model has to go into such great detail because primary factors – where market prices have the best chances to fail – play such a dominating role in many sections of the economy, as we remarked before. Here lies the main difficulty of establishing shadow prices: a detailed analysis requires a large number of *detailed statistics* and these are often only scantily available, if at all, especially in developing countries.

Thus, full analyses are hardly ever undertaken. Mostly the estimates are no more than educated guesses of the order of magnitude. Rather than go through a complicated procedure with a result that may be subject to a considerable margin of error, one simply adds a fraction to, or subtracts a fraction from the market price. This fraction of course should express the extent by which the actual price under or overvalues the underlying scarcity. This is clearly an arbitrary decision, but then it is probably better than no correction at all. For the same reason, CHAKRAVARTY[15] argues that even aggregated models may be useful for the derivation of approximative shadow prices.

A rough indication of the extent of undervaluation can be obtained from the markets which are not subject to licences, or markets which escape them, such as *black markets*. This indication can only be very crude indeed, as these markets involve only a part of supply and demand. They often also function under primitive conditions with bad communications. Finally and most important, black market prices incorporate the risk of detection, where the magnitude of the surcharge depends also on which of the two sides of the market is discouraged most: supply or demand. It is another example of the ironic effects of price intervention that one may have to turn to illegal institutions for an assessment of the extent of the deviation it brings about.

In a few rare cases, estimates of shadow prices have indeed been made, although rather in the way of a by-product as a part of the solution of a *linear programming* exercise[16]. It is well known nowadays that the solu-

15. See S. CHAKRAVARTY, 1964.
16. An exception is presented by G. SIMON, 1970. His study is exclusively concerned with the derivation and analysis of shadow prices relating to the Hungarian economy.

tion of a linear programming problem consists of two parts: the primal and the dual solution. One of the two – which one depends on the formulation of the problem – can be interpreted as the magnitude solution and the other as the price solution. Planners are often more interested in the magnitude solution which gives them a direct indication of the optimal situation they are aiming at, with a specification of the extent to which the built-in instruments have to be applied. The price solution – which we shall from now on assume to be the dual solution – is then mostly used for illustration purposes[17], where it is conveniently assumed that these dual prices coincide with shadow prices. Whether this assumption is warranted, remains to be seen, however.

Approximative procedures other than linear programming have been proposed by S. CHAKRAVARTY, *ibid.*, among others, for shadow prices of capital and foreign exchange and by I. M. D. LITTLE and J. A. MIRRLEES, 1969. A comprehensive discussion of a number of methods which concentrate on the rate of exchange has also been presented by E. BACHA and L. TAYLOR, 1971.

The quality of such methods will also depend on the question whether or not they lead to consistent shadow prices. There are, namely, two dangers in the practice of shadow pricing which are naturally underlined here, because they are directly related with the two aspects of the price consistency of a development plan which were mentioned above. The first has to do with the fact that all actual economic data incorporate the inadequacies of the prevailing price system. This implies that shadow prices would undergo the influence of – what HICKS calls – false market prices, if they were determined directly on the basis of parameters derived from actual observations. The second danger relates to the requirement that shadow prices must indeed be effectuated; shadow prices should, in other words, be employed by the economic actors when they make their decisions and not only by planners. These matters will be dealt with further in the next section and in the next chapter.

2.6. THE DIFFERENCE BETWEEN DUAL PRICES AND SHADOW PRICES

Above we have seen what the purpose of shadow prices is: they are to avoid or reduce sub-optimal allocation of resources by providing the

17. For a lucid discussion of the use of shadow prices for planning purposes, see M. BRUNO, 1967.

means for a proper evaluation of factors, goods and activities. As they do so by truly reflecting relative scarcities, obviously shadow prices must clear the market: at these prices demand must equate supply (excepting zero prices). This *equilibrating* quality has indeed been acknowledged specifically in the literature in the early stage of the discussion[18], but the property has often been ignored in subsequent writings. It will be argued here that this omission has obstructed the correct interpretation and use of shadow prices, which will prove to be of importance, not only for practical evaluation problems in which these prices are most commonly used, but also for many other planning problems, and specifically for those applying linear programming techniques.

Towards the end of the previous section, attention was drawn to the price solution in a linear programming problem. The dual prices obtained in such solutions reflect an optimal situation of which they are the counterpart. In fact, these prices are optimal prices in the sense that a corresponding evaluation leads automatically to an optimal situation, in which only activities which just break even should be allowed to operate, whereas the others which would incur a loss, should be left aside. On the other hand, shadow prices are specifically designed to obtain optimal allocation, so would it not be logical to conclude that the two are the same? In other words, would it not be sufficient to calculate the corresponding *dual* prices in a linear programming simulation of an economy, or a part of it, in order to determine a desired set of *shadow* prices? The answer is *no*, contrary to what is often suggested. Only in special cases will the two coincide, and it must at least be tested whether such a case occurs before identity of dual and shadow prices can be ascertained. For this reason we shall from now on distinguish carefully between 'dual prices' (prices in the dual solution of a linear programming problem) and 'shadow prices'.

In order to clarify this point, let us examine how dual prices are obtained. After the general structure of the model has been determined, (the economic actors, activities, resources and objective that are relevant for the particular problem to be treated, and the type of relations linking them), the coefficients must be estimated indicating to what extent a change in one item will affect other items. Also the magnitude of available resources and possibly other terms must be estimated. The way in which these parameters can be assessed may be more or less sophisticated, but, practically, they are all based on an interpretation of *actual observations*,

---

18. For example O. LANGE, *ibid.*, ch. 3 and J. TINBERGEN, 1958, p. 40. The point has also been made in S. CHAKRAVARTY, *ibid.*

25

while taking into account, of course, exogenous factors where these may play a significant role, such as, for example, a policy change, a market disruption, and so on.

Here it must be noted again that the actual observations regarding economic structure and behaviour are partly also determined by *actual prices*. Hence, the pattern which the parameters reflect bears the traces of the market prices and the same necessarily holds for the solution of the problem in which the parameters appear. It follows that the dual prices, as they are derived from a linear programming formulation, incorporate to a certain extent the defects of the false prices observed in reality which they are meant to correct.

The problem involved can also be formulated differently by saying that the parameters in the model reflect a set of market prices, whereas the solution to the same problem assumes that another set of prices (the dual prices) holds true which will not necessarily be the same as the former. In fact, there is no *a priori* reason to expect that these two sets will be identical. Hence, an inconsistency has apparently slipped in.

The root of this evil lies in the fact that there is no guarantee that dual prices conform with an *equilibrium* situation. An example may be helpful in clarifying this matter. In many linear programming exercises relating to developing countries it is found that the dual wage rate equals zero. This result is obtained if, *given the parameters which are assumed to hold*, the available labour force cannot be employed fully and profitably even if labour is paid a wage of zero. But, evidently, this is not a satisfactory conclusion, for the parameters – for example, the labour input-coefficients in a multi-sector model – have all been measured at a market wage significantly different from zero. Suppose for a moment that it were possible to estimate the values of the parameters under a wage of zero – ignoring the fact that income of wage earners would then also become nil. It would seem reasonable to expect that demand for labour would increase very considerably; demand at that price might conceivably surpass supply too, so that the dual wage rate with the new set of parameters would become positive. If that occurred, the conclusion would be that the dual wage of zero is not in equilibrium, since if it were, the demand for and supply of labour at that rate would generate again the same price. In that case also no inconsistency would have occurred, since the price of labour in the parameter set would have been the same as the dual wage in the solution.

A similar argument can be developed for, say, the rate of exchange. The dual price of foreign currency is often found to be higher than the official exchange rate. Nevertheless the relevant parameters in linear programming exercises are commonly based on the official rate. If, on the other hand, the dual rate were employed to evaluate, for example, export opportunities, the result may well be that they have increased in comparison with the original situation. And, further, if it were profitable to exploit these new opportunities, the scarcity of foreign exchange would clearly be reduced, which would, in turn, be reflected in a decrease in the new dual rate. Hence, the first dual price of foreign exchange would have appeared not to be in equilibrium.

The conclusion we can derive from the above train of thought is an important one; for it turns out that the equilibrating quality inherent in shadow prices must *also* be incorporated in dual prices in linear programming solutions if the latter are to be consistent. Further, dual prices prove not to be identical to shadow prices as long as they fail to represent an equilibrium situation, or, more precisely still, a dual solution is indeed strictly in equilibrium as long as it is derived within the framework of a restricted formulation which excludes price-quantity relations. But it is an *irrelevant* equilibrium for the same reason, if these relations have a significant impact. In that case, and in contrast with the shadow prices, the dual solution does not coincide with a situation of general equilibrium.

At first sight, this may seem to be a strange result: two sets of optimal prices which do not necessarily coincide. It springs, of course, from our observation that dual prices are optimal under the rule of a different set of prices (market prices), whereas shadow prices are optimal *and* internally consistent. The latter are, therefore, clearly superior.

It must be emphasized here that the relevance of this conclusion is not limited to the price solution in programming problems, *but extends to the primal solution* as well owing to the uniqueness of the relation between the two: deficiencies in one solution apply also to the other. Consequently even if one is interested only in the magnitude solution, it will be necessary to examine whether the dual prices are in equilibrium in order to determine its consistency. This observation explains why the importance of shadow prices goes far beyond its application in evaluation problems.

For the sake of convenience, the above reasoning has been developed on the basis of a linear programming formulation, since it brings out the price aspect of planning problems more clearly than would other approaches. However, this should not leave the impression that the critical remarks formulated here apply exclusively to problems which use this technique. In brief anticipation of a discussion of the role of prices in development planning, we must, therefore, point out even at this stage that the validity of the present arguments extends beyond the narrow frame of reference adopted in this section.

27

3. The application of shadow prices

3.1. INTRODUCTION

The concept of shadow prices arose from the apparent deficiencies of market prices, being devised in order to repair or reduce the harm that has been done in terms of misallocation of resources. It would even be better to prevent such harm, or, as TINBERGEN[1] writes: '(the best policy is one which eliminates the difference between market prices and accounting prices) according to the central proposition of free exchange, but only for markets where those conditions are fulfilled under which free exchange can work and exert its favourable influence'. In all other markets some degree of market regulation or intervention will be required. In the previous chapter it has been argued that some of the most important markets, namely those of prime factors, operate sub-optimally in most developing countries, if they are left free. Hence, there seemed to be much scope for the application of shadow prices as a device for market regulation. It may therefore be surprising that shadow prices have not reached wide-spread application. In fact, although prices observed in reality are often widely off the mark, even crude approximations of shadow prices or systems with similar results are only *rarely* imposed.

There are various reasons for this apparent aversion. The explanation will partly lie in the rather *sophisticated rationale* of shadow prices. Although it may be quite evident for the economist, the non-specialist may not like what seems to be a complicated reasoning and will tend to find it 'too theoretical'. This, in fact, is partly true. We have already observed that shadow prices can only be obtained from simulated reality and their reliability depends greatly on the degree of realism of the model used and the data put into it. The necessarily extensive character of the model provides ample opportunity for a failure on both points. Thus,

---

1. J. TINBERGEN, 1956, p. 181.

STOLPER[2] concludes '... although it is impossible to deny the imperfections of reality, the methods of improving on it may be so dubious that they lose much of their practical appeal'. Such observations, correct as they are, are not likely to inspire confidence among non-specialists, whose opinion, however, is very important, because they may play a decisive role when application of a policy is decided upon. On the other hand, one might say, that even a rather crude estimate of the true prices may well lead to a better result than actual market prices which are grossly wrong.

It can also be argued that the concept of shadow prices may be costly to apply because it will require an administrative institution to carry out the function of a shadow market and to see to it that its rules are obeyed[3]. This will depend very much on the type of procedure selected.

Next to these arguments there are a few others deserving closer attention, that go some way towards disqualifying shadow prices as an effective and practical means leading to a better allocation of scarce resources. They will be discussed after a short examination of procedures that can be adopted for the application of shadow prices. All this will serve to demonstrate why shadow prices or even crude approximations cannot easily be applied, in part or in full, in practical cases, even if the difference with market prices may be expected to be large. The treatment of dual prices in mathematical programming formulations of planning problems will, for instance, be affected by these considerations.

3.2. MEANS TO IMPOSE SHADOW PRICES

In the foregoing chapter, one approach that may possibly lead towards a more efficient distribution was mentioned, namely a *licence system*. Under such a system a central body collects applications for the use of one or more licenced factors and/or products, evaluates the applications and issues licences accordingly. Alternatively, if the commodity is in excess supply, it may allot production permits on the basis of its evaluation. Shadow prices are used only in the evaluation stage. If they are properly determined, the result of the evaluation is that the amount of resources used is exactly equal to the amount available. It will further show that, for the applications which are accepted, revenues equal costs, whereas the rejected applications would all have operated at a loss.

2. W. F. STOLPER, *ibid.*, p. 83.
3. See, for example, K. J. ARROW, 1959.

Excess profits (profits over and above 'normal profits') do not occur in this evaluation, because they would indicate either overvalued revenue or undervalued costs or both, which is not in accordance with an optimal situation.

Under this system the shadow prices never become real prices even though they should lead to a situation completely different from the one that would otherwise have existed. The prices which are actually paid and received are different. Those firms which have successfully applied for the factors, or the products of which the shadow prices turn out to be higher than the actual prices will make an excess profit, because they would have broken even at higher costs. This may be precisely the purpose of the government's price policy, if it wants to stimulate industrialization. The same reasoning applies to the sellers of products[4] with an overvalued market price. There are no special problems here.

On the other hand, however, firms evaluated positively under shadow prices and which sell undervalued products and/or buy overvalued products or factors would tend to operate at a *loss*. Such a situation cannot last in a market economy. And if the buyers are consumers, their demand for overpriced products will be smaller than it would have been if the shadow price had prevailed. Difficulties of this nature do not arise only if demand for the overpriced factors or products and supply of the underpriced factors or products are perfectly price inelastic. This is not such an academic case as it may seem, for as we have already observed above, the supply of capital hardly reacts to variations in the interest rate. CHANDAVARKAR[5] has indeed found a positive correlation between household savings and the interest rate in Taiwan and South Korea, but, generally speaking, the contribution of households to domestic savings is relatively small. Savings by enterprises and the public sector depend on other factors, and the same holds for the supply of foreign capital, where the possibility of transfer of profits and the risk of devaluation and nationalization are important determinants which reduce the influence of the interest rate. Although important, this is an isolated case, however; price inelasticity may not be assumed to hold generally.

In short, with an exception for capital, a simple rationing system such as described above will not work. The basic reason is that it may be possible to *curtail* the side of the market that makes an *excess profit* (the long side of the market) by rationing the use of undervalued items and

4. Suppliers of prime factors – practically only wage earners in a situation of severe unemployment – do not make an 'excess profit' and have therefore not been included.
5. A. G. CHANDAVARKAR, 1970.

the production of overvalued items, but that its counterpart, the *short side*, will tend to buy or sell *less* than the amounts corresponding with the shadow price. These amounts can only be realised if the latter is made effective with the help of subsidies, thereby raising demand for the overvalued product and supply of the undervalued good.

Another way out might seem to be to accept the levels at the short side of the market at the prevailing market prices and to limit the side that is in excess accordingly by applying a 'shadow price' that reduces the long side sufficiently. The distribution of licences could then be based on an evaluation according to these prices. A situation like this, where the short side of the market dictates the magnitude exchanged, is in general not an optimum and will not necessarily be much of an improvement as compared with the original market situation. Consequently, it is all the more remarkable to find that programming models are commonly built according to this principle. The consequences thereof will be discussed extensively below.

Apparently a licence system without complementary subsidies which render the shadow prices operational is not an effective proposition. A next step might be to abolish the licences completely and replace them by taxes that raise the price of undervalued products and factors and reduce profits on overvalued products. (Also here it may be inappropriate to talk about 'profits' if the overpriced goods help to earn a mere subsistence income for those who depend on them.) Ideally, the resulting market situation would be exactly the same as under shadow prices.

A *tax/subsidy system* differs in two aspects from the licence/subsidy system. In the former, excess profits will not occur, they are taxed away. If applied, it will tend to cover the entire economy, whereas the licence/ subsidy system will be better suited for new projects only. It is also conceivable that the tax/subsidy system be applied exclusively to new ventures[6], but the practical difficulties will be very great. For example, it will be very hard to distinguish between old and new when an existing plant is enlarged.

On the other hand, if the tax/subsidy system is applied to the economy as a whole there will probably be a number of projects which were profitable under the original market prices, but which will now swing into the red. If the system were pushed through rigorously, the economy would inevitably incur a loss, since resources used in the uneconomic lines cannot always be easily shifted to profitable ones. Therefore, it seems to pay not to be too strict, though it will be hard to draw a dividing

6. See A. QAYUM, 1960.

line. This is only one of the difficulties to be encountered when it comes to actual application of shadow prices. The next section will discuss some even more critical remarks.

3.3. RESTRICTIONS TO PRACTICAL APPLICABILITY

We have seen above that a policy of redressing the effects of false prices with the help of a licence system that seems, at first sight not to have financial repercussions, still requires supplementary *subsidies* to function properly. The use of public financial means is even explicitly present in the alternative tax/subsidy system. Criticism regarding the practical application of shadow prices is essentially aimed against this property.

3.3.1. Financial complications

In developing countries the financing of state activities is a particularly great problem. The low level of economic development aggravates the problem in a number of ways. There is first the obvious difficulty that income and sales taxes will contribute relatively little if the level of economic activity is low. Only a small margin is available for taxation. It is true that there are components of public revenue which have a minimum impact on the poor and the very poor, such as wealth and property taxes, duties and taxes on luxury goods, etc., but the opportunities for taxation are thus severely limited.

Other factors, also on the side of public revenue, are the rather low administrative efficiency in developing countries and the difficulty of tax collection in the non-monetized sector. With bad communications and non-existent or incomplete registration of population and economic activities, available sources of government income, being unnoticed, remain untapped. The sources themselves will not offer help to change this situation and will rather do whatever they can to let it persist. And even after being identified as a taxable entity, the system will lend opportunities for evasion. This also helps to explain why public revenues in developing countries rely to a great extent on import duties (often between forty and seventy per cent of total tax revenues)[7]. Imported goods are relatively easy to trace and, thus, become an obvious target.

On the other hand, the tasks of governments in developing countries are manifold and costly. To initiate or speed up growth in a stagnant,

7. See B. NOWZAD, 1969.

low-income economy constitutes a very complex problem which may require, for example, the build-up of the infrastructure – an extremely capital-intensive affair. Or, in order to ensure future growth, an expansion of the educational system may be necessary which will only become productive a decade later. Further, it may be considered desirable to establish state enterprises requiring public investments, so as to set the pace of the industrialization process.

With such a heavy structural strain on the public budget, where urgent expenditures are to be financed out of very limited revenues, it is not difficult to predict the reaction to a request for public funds, or for a very drastic change in the tax system in connection with something so intangible and 'theoretical' as shadow prices. Even under more favourable circumstances than those prevailing in the developing world, it would be difficult to use the structure of public finances as an instrument to attain true prices and a better resource allocation, especially because the taxes and subsidies have to be pinpointed with great precision. With the practical obstructions mentioned above and the impressive magnitudes involved, it will *often* be *practically impossible* in underdeveloped countries.

However, the situation should not be left as it is. Any organization that shares responsibility for the state of the economy, in which prices do not properly reflect scarcities, will be aware that there is a strong tendency for the underpriced resources to be in excess demand, whereas the overpriced resources will remain underutilized. They should lean against this trend and we have already noted that there is indeed room for doing so. This policy will probably be better than nothing at all.

A point raised by STOLPER and later by P. ECKSTEIN[8] relates to a situation where the government has indeed public funds available for subsidies to be distributed according to the shadow-price principle. Two cases should now be compared, namely on the one hand the increase in welfare obtained from a *better use of resources* thanks to an improvement of the price system after taking into account the costs involved by its organization, with, on the other hand, the increase in welfare resulting from *investment of the funds*. Although it has not been indicated according to which prices – market or shadow prices – these funds should be allocated, the argument is clear enough. And even if the comparison has never actually been made, it is understandable that an institution confronted with the choice would play it safe and invest.

---

8. P. ECKSTEIN, 1968.

3.3.2. Administrative complications

In order to make this discussion a little less abstract, let us investigate the *magnitudes of taxes and subsidies* that may be involved, although this can only be done very tentatively. For example, let us assume that a country's capital coefficient (physical capital to national income) is 2.5 years, and, further, that the difference between the market rate of interest and the shadow rate is ten per cent. These figures would imply that an amount equal to twenty-five per cent of national income would have to be taxed away from capital users in order to correct the false price of capital.

On the other hand, since the shadow price of labour will be lower than the actual price, subsidies will have to be paid to employers of labour. If we take a labour force of forty per cent of the total population of which eighty per cent is unskilled, and a difference between market wage and shadow wage of unskilled labour equal to two-thirds of income per capita, these subsidies would amount to some twenty-one per cent of national income.

Of course, for a proper evaluation of the difficulties involved we must realize that a relatively small portion of these sums will actually have to change hands, since there will be much scope for internal compensation of taxes to be received from and subsidies to be paid to the same agents. However, the combination of the impressive magnitudes of the sums which are at stake and the weak central administrative machinery which is to control them would render the whole operation hazardous.

This is also why it is not enough to examine exclusively the net financial implications of shadow pricing for the public budget, as QAYUM does. The net financial burden is not representative of the task the state faces when applying a policy of shadow prices. On balance, of course, the tax or subsidy flow may appear to be of manageable proportions, but it hides the *absolute* size of the funds which have to be administered and controlled in the process. It is precisely this technical aspect which endangers the success of such an operation to an extent which probably goes a long way to explain the lack of popularity of shadow pricing.

For example, QAYUM finds in an exercise that, given the values of parameters in his model, a net additional amount of taxes of, at most, only three per cent of national income will be required in order to finance a shadow-price policy[9]. (In our example above, the policy would even be advantageous to the state, since it would accrue a rise of net

9. *Ibid.*, p. 88 *et seq.*

public revenue by about four per cent of national income.) But it can easily be calculated that this net burden results from subsidy and tax flows of 18.5 and 15.5 per cent of national income respectively. These volumes[10] are more representative of the magnitude of the administrative problem.

Because of the inelasticity with respect to fluctuations of the rate of interest, subsidies on capital supply will not have a significant effect and will therefore not be necessary. On the other hand, taxation of capital usage would eliminate the industrialization incentive and would be attractive only from the point of view of tax collection. In fact, the reason why capital taxes have been included in the example is precisely to examine how far they may go to finance labour subsidies.

It is true that the sums derived here *exaggerate* the amounts that will actually be needed. Firstly, shadow pricing in the *subsistence sector* does not seem to be a practical proposition, so a considerable portion of many developing economies can be left out of consideration. Secondly, there may be cases where the price ratio is of little importance, namely, in those sectors which do *not* face *competition from abroad* and where only *one technique* of production is available. Domestic demand for goods from such sectors (national sectors, see section 2.2. above) can only be satisfied by domestic production and, hence, neither the choice between imports and domestic production, nor the choice between techniques arises. But sectors which possess these properties, except, perhaps, the public administration and education sectors, will be hard to find. One remaining difficulty may still be that at the ruling market prices production may still be too high or too low in comparison with the volumes produced under shadow prices. In that case it may still be necessary to levy taxes or grant subsidies in order to reach the desired activity levels.

Another consideration with the effect of reducing the need for intervention derives from the fact that the subsistence-wage level may conceivably fall when the employment level rises. The unemployed who used to depend on the employed workers – a common phenomenon in

---

10. QAYUM's figures probably tend to be on the low side due to the COBB-DOUGLAS production function he applies. Let L and K indicate the amounts of labour and capital available and $\bar{L}$ and $\bar{K}$ the volumes actually employed. The market wage would thus become $\bar{w} = a\bar{L}^{a-1}\bar{K}^{1-a}$ and the shadow wage $w^0 = aL^{a-1}K^{1-a}$. Assuming that $K = \bar{K}$ and $\bar{L} = cL$ $(0 < c < 1)$ one finds that $w^0 = \dfrac{1}{c^{a-1}}\bar{w}$. If $a = .75$ and with thirty per cent unemployment, the shadow wage would still be more than ninety per cent of the market wage, which seems to be much higher than is normally assumed.

developing countries – will earn their own income after labour has been subsidized, resulting in an increased demand for labour. Now the wage rate per worker can decrease without reducing the level of material well-being of the unskilled manpower population, since the average number of *dependants per wage earner* will have *dropped* substantially. Evidently, the extent of the reduction will be correlated with the improvement of the employment situation.

In the above example, in which the parameters are hypothetical, there is no sense in speculating how much will still be needed in terms of taxes and subsidies after these corrections. The amounts are so large, however, that even a very significant reduction would still not render a full application of the shadow-price principle through the tax/subsidy system feasible. The possible errors due to shortcomings of the administrating body and the large-scale fraud it invites, may do more harm than good.

There may be other, less costly policies to bring the unemployment problem closer to a solution. The government may, for example, offer additional employment opportunities by increasing the scale of its economic activities. Infrastructure projects may indeed be well designed for this purpose[11]. In this way unused labour resources are made productive, which is a good thing, but the effects are limited to the public sector; the combinations in which prime factors are employed in the private sector remain the same.

It is more important to emphasize however that there is still scope for an attack on unemployment. Even though the immediate opportunities for achieving higher rates of employment seem to be rather few (see subsection 2.2.2.), the potential effects from a cross-sectoral shift towards more labour-intensive technologies are certainly impressive.

3.4. PROPER USE OF SHADOW PRICES AND CONCLUSIONS

Our discussion of the characteristics of shadow prices of the three primary factors has shown that they differ from each other when it comes to practical application. We have seen that it is not really necessary to impose the shadow price of capital in order to improve the functioning of the market mechanism because of the insensitivity of supply (the short side of the market) to a price change. It would be sufficient to distribute among users according to a criterion that reflects the shadow rate of interest. A system of licences will suffice, special tax or subsidy measures are not required.

11. See R. NURKSE, 1961 and J. P. LEWIS, 1972.

36

The picture is different for the rate of foreign exchange: both exports and imports may be expected to vary with the price of foreign currency, although in many developing countries imports of a number of products will be subject to quantitative restrictions and, consequently, insensitive to price changes. But even in this case an adjustment of the exchange rate may be corrective by eliminating simultaneously the upward pressure on imports and the reason for the existence of the black exchange market. So if the shadow rate differs significantly from the official rate certain measures would be desirable. They may consist either of a combination of taxes and subsidies on imports and exports respectively, or of an appropriate change in the official price of foreign exchange. These two alternatives can be considered as substitutes for our purposes here, although the implications for a country's financial structure can be vastly different (see R. SOLIGO, 1971). But a devaluation has great advantages as it requires much less effort, especially in the long run. The main obstacle is often the devaluphobia of the policy makers.

Real difficulties arise only when it comes to the effectuation of the shadow wage. It seems likely that the amount of financial resources required for this purpose tends to be out of proportion with the financial capacities of developing countries. The same may apply to products for which the application of shadow prices is contemplated. As there may be no way out, this implies that there are circumstances which prohibit the execution of a labour-market policy based on the shadow wage. The same conclusion applies of course to other markets for which large sums and great precision in the execution are needed to redress a sub-optimal situation. It is good to remember though that still other markets exist where these problems do not occur.

Thus we are led to an important conclusion pointed out earlier by MOUSTACCHI[12], which is that the *practical limits* of a *price policy* must be taken into account in those problems where other than market prices are involved. Although this remark may seem self-evident, it is made here with some emphasis, because it is nevertheless often neglected. The result of such neglect in all cases where prices occur explicitly or implicitly is obviously that one loses touch with reality. Two fields seem to be particularly vulnerable, namely those where shadow prices play an important role: evaluation studies and programming problems. However, it will be argued subsequently that the problem may occur in other areas as well.

Suppose that in an appraisal of the social profitability of a number of projects a set of prices is applied that deviates from the set of prices used

12. M. MOUSTACCHI, 1965.

in real transactions. The question now is what will happen to projects which were found to be profitable under the accounting prices, after they are implemented, if the government is not able to effectuate these prices. The answer has been given already: some ventures will make an unexpectedly large profit and others will operate at an unforeseen loss, depending on whether the difference between the two price sets is on balance in their favour, or not. Since the actual outcome is different anyway from the results one is aiming at, the effort will have been rather useless.

Although this type of error can indeed be observed from time to time in practical evaluations, the number of misjudgements it has given rise to is hard to guess. Probably it will not have reached large proportions, since, firstly, appraisals in the private sector are naturally based on market prices, secondly, shadow prices are used only rather rarely as we have mentioned already and, thirdly, the actual profitability does not necessarily compare unfavourably with the estimated outcome although the contrary is more probable. But even if the error has remained relatively unimportant, this is by virtue of external circumstances and *not* in any way an achievement of the theory and practice of development planning.

The conclusion is different for linear programming problems, however, because dual prices are an integrating part of them. If they differ from the actual price set – which is highly likely in development planning – the danger of overreaching the constraints of the official price policy becomes very real. Clearly, this difficulty can be solved very easily by introducing *bounds* for the minimum and/or maximum levels that dual prices may reach. By doing so the dual solution can be checked to remain within a reasonable distance of the actual price range. It need not be emphasized that the corresponding primal solution may differ widely from the solution in the absence of price constraints.

Perhaps it is worth stressing once more that the above is not meant as a warning against the use of shadow prices. Rather it warns against incorrect use of shadow prices that would lead to an invalid judgement when they do not agree with a price-consistent plan. This is also what MYRDAL is driving at in his definition of 'planned prices'[13]. It is therefore surprising to find that he is highly critical of shadow prices. Part of the reason resides in the fact that he incorrectly attributes to the concept of

13. 'Planned prices ... are those prices that, under all existing conditions including the full range of government policies, would give entrepreneurs and, more generally, producers, traders, consumers, and savers incentives to act according to a particular development plan' (G. MYRDAL, 1968, p. 2037).

equilibrium a metaphysical quality which he abhors. However, the adjustment process by which the planned prices are to be attained according to MYRDAL is, in point of fact, an equilibrium process. For this reason also shadow prices are no more 'indeterminate' than planned prices, and, in my view, the similarity between the two concepts stands out rather than the difference, if there is one.

So when working with shadow prices one should keep two points in mind: they should be *stable* – which is short for saying that their application should not bear in itself forces leading towards a new situation where these prices are no longer valid, see the previous chapter – and they should be *realistic* – which means that they should remain within the price range that the government can implement and control. Both conditions are to be met simultaneously; otherwise the significance of an exercise for practical purposes would be seriously reduced. Neither a stable, but unrealistic set of prices, nor an unstable, but realistic system will be a dependable guide in economic planning and the same holds for any set of values that is directly linked with either of the two. This is a rather unpleasant conclusion, because the planner's job is difficult enough without taking into account these complications. Nevertheless, allowance will have to be made for it so as to avoid an incorrect outline of the course a nation is to follow to achieve its development aims. A situation characterized by a price system that is both stable and realistic is *price consistent*.

Again the planner may find himself in a somewhat awkward position when he is to apply a system of prices that he considers inappropriate. He is not powerless though; he can and should make his arguments known to the institutions authorized to decide on and execute the price policy. The opinion of the planner whose main concern is the economic and social development of a country, should weigh heavily wherever a high priority is attached to an improvement in national well-being. Needless to add that his views should reflect a reasonable assessment of the limitations of price manipulations. But we have seen that there are some classes of factors where effective prices can be altered without great difficulty. If the functioning of an economy can be improved by adopting a scarcity-oriented price policy, as a policy based on shadow prices should be capable of doing, without creating social injustice, the only obstacle which may remain may be the costs of executing it. The case for shadow prices would therefore be greatly strengthened if an estimate of the costs could be confronted with a quantitative evaluation of the benefits that will result. It will be seen below, however, that this task will not be an easy one to fulfil. In the near future the arguments in favour of shadow prices will therefore probably continue to draw mainly on rather theoretical reasoning and, at best, crude guesses of cost and benefits.

If planners cannot convince the authorities concerned and a price set is accepted different from the one they proposed, they have no choice but to work with it. They should see to it that the plan is entirely consistent with the actual prices even if the planners' proposition is considered to be better. For if this proposition did not convince the other party, it implies that the planners applied a different criterion, which brings us back to the question of the acceptability of the state's welfare function which was mentioned in the previous chapter. However, a plan would be turned into a purely theoretical exercise, if it reflected a set of prices that does not correspond with the actual price policy. In that case, it has little practical significance and its outcome would make poor planning, or in a paraphrase of Marshall BOSQUET's comment on the charging Light Brigade: *C'est magnifique, mais ce n'est pas la planification.*

4. Price consistency and economic planning

4.1. THE TRADITIONAL ROLE OF PRICES IN PLANNING MODELS

In this chapter the effects will be discussed of an application of the price-consistency concept in economic planning. As before we shall distinguish between two aspects of the concept, namely, (i) the necessity to establish equilibrium between prices and quantities, and (ii) the limitations to price variations in reality.

The question which role prices play in economic planning is subordinate to the more general question of what economic planning intends to achieve. So let us consider the latter's purposes as a starting point for an analysis of what one may reasonably expect of prices in this context. In a few words, *economic planning* may be said to aim at the achievement of a certain objective in one or more variables acting as welfare indicators, while taking into account a number of constraints describing the functioning of an economy and bearing a certain relation with the variables in the objective function, in as far as these are directly or indirectly influenced by the constraints.

Given the fact that planning makes sense only for a future period when there is still scope for a certain degree of manipulation, the following elements play a very prominent role, (i) the *predictive* element (relating to factors that cannot, or cannot easily be controlled), (ii) the *indicative* element (indicating the aims to be reached during the period under consideration), (iii) the *manipulative* element (the measures that have to be taken in order to reach the goals). An economic plan should clearly be formulated in such a way that it takes these elements satisfactorily into account. The conglomerate of objectives, identification of the relevant economic framework, and the instruments and policy measures that have to be applied together constitute the plan.

Essentially the constraints describe the economic constellation within which the objectives must be realized. They may be technical relations indicating the possibilities and limitations of available techniques, or they may be behavioural relations, which lay down the pattern of behaviour of the relevant economic participants. There may also be some equations which are neither behavioural nor technical, whose purpose it is to knit the system together; they may be called accounting equations.

It is true that the above description of an economic plan suggests the presence of an algebraic planning model in the background, where terms like 'objective' and 'constraints' hint at a mathematical-programming formulation. For reasons of efficiency which will be indicated sub-sequently, our analysis will indeed be based on such a model, but, on the other hand, it is important to realize that the roles of prices in economic planning as it will be described here are not specifically tied to this special formulation.

Economic planning may also be carried out without the aid of an algebraic model in the background, although in this way planning in some detail will soon become extremely difficult. Further, planning without figures is not really possible[1]; some degree of quantification is indispensable. And since any logical reasoning involving quantitative expressions can be formulated as a system of algebraic relations, such a system or model may be a useful tool in economic planning, if only because it reduces the danger of inherent inconsistencies that an economic plan may otherwise display. Evidently, applications are limited to quan-tifiable variables and remain approximations of actual relationships and, therefore, algebraic models of socio-economic reality should never replace entirely the insider's independent judgement. However, the misunder-standing that, even after correcting for this consideration, a 'mathematical approach' to economic planning somehow changes the nature of the problem and leads to interpretations and conclusions different from the other approach which shuns mathematics, is strangely persistent. Instead, a mathematical treatment can be regarded as an alternative language which will often facilitate a better understanding of a problem if its limitations are kept in mind. It follows that, if there is a difference between the two approaches, this will more likely than not be in favour of the one which also employs a mathematical interpretation. In any case, when reference is made below to a planning model, the conclusions extend to other approaches to planning that can be represented by such a model.

With sufficient knowledge of the social, political and economic structure (including resources) of a country and an assessment of relevant future developments (such as export opportunities, the composition of domestic demand, foreign aid, etc.) and given the development objectives, a

---

1. This has been clearly demonstrated by W. F. STOLPER, *ibid.*

development strategy can be formulated. Thus, the strategy may be out-ward-looking or inward-looking, labour-using or capital-intensive, it may put emphasis on large-scale rather than small-scale industries, and so on.

When the configuration composed of these elements has been deter-mined, a number of very important conclusions can already be drawn, for one can then attempt to locate the bottle-necks that will need particular attention. If, for example, the export opportunities of a country are not very promising, if it aims at a significant reduction of its trade deficit and if the strategy adopted tends to be import-using, it is not hard to predict that foreign exchange will probably become a bottle-neck that may endanger the achievement of the objectives. In other words, its scarcity will probably rise. On the other hand, the same configuration may imply that the scarcity of, for example, unskilled labour may fall. Of course, in practice, scarcity evaluations will not be as simple as is suggested here, but the point is that the above-mentioned elements *permit* an evaluation of scarcities.

As these elements are incorporated in a plan, it follows that *a plan involves a certain pattern of scarcities* which differs with the way it has been formulated. And it is important to observe that such value patterns are implied by all types of planning models, even in those where they do not appear explicitly.

Thus, if 'scarcities' is translated into 'prices', one is led to the conclusion that what is said here on price realism, price equilibrium and price consistency with reference to development planning models formulated as programming problems, applies, in fact, to development planning *in general.* The reason why this matter is treated here within the frame-work of the *programming* type of models is simply that such models provide a directly interpretable, explicit *expression* of the valuation pattern which they imply. The very fact that prices remain obscure in other approaches may well be an explanation for the traditional neglect of prices in the practice of development planning.

It appears that, if prices are taken into account in a development plan, this is nearly always done in macro-economic terms. For example, a planning policy may include measures to stabilize the domestic price level, or an analysis may be carried out to estimate the effects of a decline of the terms of trade. Such a general treatment is, of course, perfectly acceptable, since there is no scope for more details in a macro-type approach. But this is no longer true in multi-sector planning, in which a number of prices occur, even if in a hidden form.

Just as the scarcity pattern of a plan may change with its formulation, the price solution of a programming problem may change with the formulation of that problem, and for the same reasons. Inversely, an exogenous change in this price set may necessitate another solution. Consider, for example, a simple multi-sector planning model, including an input-output part, factor-demand relations for labour, capital and foreign exchange, and upper limits for exports which force a considerable number of sectors into production[2]. Suppose that in the optimal solution the foreign exchange constraint is binding and the labour constraint is not, with a positive dual price for the first factor and a zero price for the other factor. The price pattern in the dual solution is such that the sectors with positive production volumes in the optimal solution just break even (revenues equal to costs), where other sectors would operate at a loss at these prices and, therefore, do not produce. In other words, the dual prices (which are optimal prices under the given parameter set), can also be used to select the sectors appearing in the optimal solution. The simplex method using multipliers is based on precisely this property.

Now suppose that the prices are autonomously fixed at a different level, say, the wage rate is increased and the rate of exchange is forced down compared with the initial dual prices. Clearly the selection process may now end up with a different result: sectors with a higher foreign exchange input and a lower labour input than those originally in the basis now become more profitable propositions, and may cause a change in the pattern of production.

This is, in fact, what happens if binding price restrictions are added to the model and a deviation from the restriction-free dual prices is required. In chapter 3 we indicated extensively why it may not be possible to effectuate shadow prices, if they differ widely from the actual market prices. A drastic restriction of the range of price variation is, therefore, more probable than not in the real world, and a planning model should take account of this fact in order to be realistic. As has been indicated by MOUSTACCHI, this is the *restrictive* role that prices in planning models may play.

There is still another factor which has to do with the strong relation between the optimum and the equilibrium (section 5.2.). Evidently, economic planning is concerned with optimization, but it has also been

2. For a discussion of the properties of such a model, see P. A. CORNELISSE and J. VERSLUIS, 1969.

indicated in chapter 2 that the magnitudes of the variables in the plan must be in a balanced relation with the set of prices implied by it. If not, the role of prices may be to help *steer the economy* in the adaptative process towards the constellation that the plan is aiming at (see the next chapter). A different position under the same objectives and the same constraints but not in equilibrium would display a persistent tendency in reality to break away from the planned development. In the terminology employed in the next chapter, it may be said that an economic plan should be a goal equilibrium and the prices belonging to it should, therefore, be goal-equilibrium prices, or, simply, shadow prices.

How can one determine whether the plan is in equilibrium or not? After what has been said above the answer is quite simple: if all volumes and prices employed in formulating the plan are consistent one with another (taking into account the price-quantity relations), the plan is a balanced one. But we observed in the second chapter that such a situation is unlikely to occur spontaneously in developing countries with some of their main markets in structural disequilibrium. So, an adaptation process will probably have to be carried out in order to *locate* the desired equilibrium situation. It seems worth while, therefore, to investigate further a situation, in which the price set used as a background for the original formulation of the plan, differs from the set of prices which indicate the true relative scarcities involved by the plan. This means that the prices under which the coefficients and constant terms have been determined in the corresponding programming model will *also* deviate from the prices in the dual solution. For, even though shadow prices and dual prices are not exactly the same, a difference between shadow prices and market prices implies – price restrictions apart – a difference between dual prices and market prices.

If a dual price for a factor in the optimal solution is higher than the price paid for it in the market, it obviously indicates that the model attributes a higher value to the factor *within the structure prevailing under the market prices* than reality does. And clearly, if the dual price were lower, the interpretation is that the model attaches a lower value to the factor within this structure than its actual price. In other words, dual prices point out whether inadequacies exist in a certain price system and they also indicate the direction in which an improvement can be sought. This conclusion helps to explain the role that dual prices may play as a guide towards the equilibrium point. This matter will further be elaborated upon in chapters 5 and 6.

This still leaves the question of the extent and way in which the parameters in a planning model are affected by prices. It should first be mentioned that the price dependency as it is meant here, does not relate to the fact that many parameters in planning models are value-magnitudes (price times quantity) in which prices appear as components and therefore influence the level of these values directly. Rather it refers to the relation between prices and quantities through which the parameters are affected if prices change, even if they are expressed in constant prices. The difficulty of a general treatment of this relation is here that the formulation of a model (the variables occurring in it, the shape of the functions relating them, and therefore, also the parameters appearing in the model) depends strongly on the purpose that the model serves and on practical limitations as regards, for example, data availability. Thus there are quite a few types of models, each with innumerable variants which suggests that it is impossible to generalize on the impact of prices on parameters without reference to a specific model.

But even considering this, it can be maintained that only very few parameters in economic models will be completely *insensitive* to the price environment, simply because there are hardly any items in the economic world which possess this property. In fact, only input coefficients in optimization problems that select between different techniques (see the numerical example in the next chapter) would seem to belong to this category. Problems dealing with this type of information are, in fact, meant to select from available alternatives expressed in physical quantities, such as production techniques. This is not the case with, for example, the coefficients of an input-output table which represent the weighted average of the techniques applied by the sectors. If prices underwent drastic changes making different production techniques with a different cost structure profitable, the original input coefficients would no longer apply. This is, at least, what one would expect. However, although the evidence is not conclusive, the international comparison of input-output tables made by CHENERY and WATANABE[3] suggests that the influence of prices is relatively small. This may be due to the limited number of available production techniques indicated above. It seems, therefore, that with the exception of input coefficients in a model that allows a choice between different production techniques, the magnitudes of all parameters in a multi-sector planning problem may, in effect, depend on prices.

3. H. B. CHENERY and T. WATANABE, 1958.

4.3. IMPLICATIONS

Let us now try to take stock of the consequences of bringing into effect these additional price considerations in actual planning problems. Doing so, we shall have to face the fact that most of them are rather unpleasant.

First, when past exercises have failed to take into account the need for internal equilibrium and/or the limitations of the range of prices in reality, they are, according to the arguments presented here, subject to *doubt* as to their practical significance. As long as the effect of these two factors on the outcomes of existing exercises has not been evaluated, it remains impossible to decide whether or not the original results are still acceptable. It is true that even if an analysis is conceptually incomplete, it may still be useful, if only the consequences of the omission are small enough to ignore. But this depends entirely on the nature of the problem; clearly, a certain concept may be of vital importance in one case, whereas it may perhaps be airily neglected in another. Generalizations are always dangerous.

It seems relevant, therefore, to investigate under which specific circumstances the price-equilibrium aspect may have no further impact on the planning analyses so far available (chapter 3 has already examined this question for the price-restriction aspect). Indeed we must speak of 'specific circumstances', because there will be at least one stage in a comprehensive planning procedure (corresponding with the 'middle phase' in planning-in-stages, see section 1.1.) where demand and supply present themselves in such an overwhelming fashion that demand and supply relations cannot be avoided. Therefore, it is really a special case if these relations are not violated, when they have not been taken into account expressly under circumstances involving very considerable price variations. Only two circumstances seem capable of giving rise to such a situation, namely, first, *price inelasticity* of demand and supply of all relevant products and factors and, second, a planned development which is in *equilibrium* with the initial situation, such that significant changes in the pattern of relative scarcities will not occur.

In the first case supply as well as demand quantities are fixed irrespective of prices and they can become equal only if the demand and supply curves – both running parallel to the price axis – happen to coincide; prices are irrelevant in this case. But such a construction, which would have to apply to all parameters clearly lacks realism, so the practical value of this possibility is very much restricted.

In the second case we have an initial situation in which all relevant prices and quantities are well-balanced one to the other, and which is expressed in the parameters of the problem. In an analysis of this situation, and if one assumes a proper representation of the actual constraints and objectives in the model, one may, thus, expect to find equilibrium values in the primal and dual solutions. Such an exercise is of course only interesting in as far as it may help to clarify the economic mechanism in the equilibrium. Planners can make use of these findings because they indicate the relevant relationships to be incorporated in the planning procedure. But planning itself is typically concerned with the future and the question remains whether the equilibrium will then still exist, which will be the case only if the original relative scarcities are not affected by the future requirements as stipulated by the plan and the alterations of the technical and behavioural relations.

It can be added that, when actual prices are in equilibrium and remain so, the question of the practical price range becomes redundant: the equilibrium prices coincide with the actual prices so their realism cannot be in doubt. The question whether a continuously smooth development path can be expected to occur on a significant scale is more important and has already been discussed above. The continuing process of structural change and, in particular, the absence of a reasonable degree of equilibrium in the poor countries are factors that tend to reduce the relevance of this second case considerably too.

Another consequence of the introduction of the price-equilibrium aspect is that a vast number of parameters, which have been ignored until now in economic planning, wil have to be made available, for an equilibrium analysis requires knowledge of the reactions of all relevant demand and supply quantities to price changes. In other words, extensive *information* is needed on price elasticities of demand and supply of products and factors of production (both direct elasticities and cross elasticities) and also on income elasticities, in as far as changes in factor prices give rise to a different income pattern. Ideally, these elasticities would express the relations between all prices playing a role in the problem and all parameters.

This conclusion is particularly unpleasant, as it requires an increase in the number of statistical estimates that have to be made before the model can be solved. Even without these additional requirements, the task of deriving satisfactory parameters is often very time-consuming, especially, again, in developing countries. Often, planners have to compile their own statistics right from the bottom, starting at the basic sources; only rarely can direct use be made of data collected and presented by other institutions (mainly on taxes and international trade). Now it appears that these laboriously determined parameters are not yet sufficient

48

and have to be complemented by still other parameters that indicate the price sensitivity of the former.

In practice it will be impossible to assess in a satisfactory way all relationships between the parameters of a model and the prices involved, if only because the immense number of data needed for this purpose cannot reasonably be expected to become available. But this will not be strictly necessary, since the vast majority of cross elasticities will not be significantly different from zero anyway. So the estimation of price and income elasticities may be limited practically to direct elasticities with only a few exceptions for factors or products where substitution or complementary effects cannot be ignored. But even after this reduction, the question remains whether these minimum requirements can be coped with satisfactorily. The present stock of price and income elasticities falls far short of the number required for the present purpose, thereby further widening the existing gap between available and required information for development planning, which is as old as development planning itself.

In addition to the augmented task during the preparatory stage, there is the increased complexity of the *solution procedure* itself. For the equilibrium dimension that we have added here to the planning procedure in its traditional form does not merely inflate the problem to a larger size, but also changes its nature. In the traditional formulation of planning problems, the solution – provided that it exists – can be directly obtained from the parameters, but in our amended approach the latter in their turn are dependent on the (price) solution. Hence, an interdependence exists between parameters and solution, rather than a one-way dependence. It will be clear that this property upsets the common solution techniques for traditional problems so that a special approach must be devised in order to tackle this new problem.

Chapter 6 will discuss a number of tentative ways to deal with the equilibrium aspects in economic planning, and briefly anticipating the conclusions presented there, we can mention now that each of them implies, as might be expected, a larger computational effort than would have been required if the equilibrium concept had been ignored, although one approach may perhaps be more efficient than the other. Following a principle that resembles very much the digestive system of ruminants, these methods tackle the same basic problem in a number of successive stages[4], where the problem changes shape in each stage until, at last, the solution has become equilibrated. Hence, the improved quality that the

---

4. The stages as they are meant here are different from the rounds of calculations that are common in linear programming algorithms.

extended problem offers by eliminating price inconsistencies, has to be paid for in terms of greater effort in its preparation and solution.

4.4. CONSEQUENCES FOR SOLUTION VALUES

What will the effects be of an application of the price-consistency concept on the outcome of the planning procedure? In what respects will a plan based on this approach differ from a plan that is formulated along the traditional lines? Will these differences show a particular tendency? Evidently these are also questions of interest to people involved in practical planning and one may wonder whether they can be answered at this stage. In this section we shall concentrate on the equilibrium aspect; the price-restriction aspect will be dealt with in section 4.5.

It will be helpful to attempt to tackle these questions again assuming that the outline of the plan refers to the solution of a programming problem designed for that purpose. Without proper measures such a problem will probably end up with an inconsistent solution expressed in a deviation of the dual prices from the prices underlying the parameters. In section 2 of this chapter it was mentioned that these dual prices may be used as indicators of the direction in which the actual prices would move in the first instance, if they were left free. This observation can be turned into a basis for a process of adaptation which simulates the development of the prices in the course of time and which may ultimately lead to the equilibrium position we are looking for (see sections 3 and 4 of the next chapter). The effects of an adaptation of the actual prices in the direction of the dual prices can be reasoned out – and then only tentatively – only if they are isolated from each other.

Suppose again that a simple multi-sector programming model, as outlined in section 2, gives a dual rate of exchange that is significantly higher than the official rate on which the parameters have been based, indicating that, according to the model, domestic currency is officially overvalued. If a higher-than-official rate were now used as a reference price, some of the parameters – especially those relating to import and export behaviour – are bound to be affected. The effect will probably be that export opportunities are expanded – expressed in the model, for example, through an increase in the upper limits of exports – whereas the propensity to import may diminish. The easing of the external trade position as compared with the original situation will result in a dual exchange rate which may be equal to or lower than the first dual rate, *but which will not be higher*. If the new dual rate is lower than the *imposed* rate of the second iteration, the rate imposed in the third iteration is to be adjusted downwards. But even in the other case, if exports and imports react to a rise in the exchange rate in the way assumed here, the price of foreign exchange in later iterations, however, will not surpass the dual rate obtained in the first iteration. The latter, therefore, may be considered as an upper limit for the equilibrium rate. So it can be concluded that under the above-mentioned conditions, the tendency, if there is one, is that the dual price in the first iteration *exaggerates* the adaptation required to achieve equilibrium.

But it must immediately be added that this conclusion is a very limited one, applying only to an isolated price adaptation and under the assumption that a price increase reduces excess demand. If the latter assumption does not apply the above reasoning is rendered invalid, whereas in the case of multiple price adaptations a straightforward conclusion is hampered by the possibility of counter-acting price developments, namely, if the indirect effects (through the interdependence of activity levels in the problem) and/or cross effects of other price changes more than counterbalance the direct effect as described in the preceding paragraph. It follows that the relation between a 'naive' plan and one that takes into account the price-consistency complication may differ from case to case and depends on the parameters of the problem, including the elasticities. But in so far as adverse effects are the exception rather than the rule, the pattern outlined above may well tend to dominate resulting in initial dual prices overestimating the price distortion. (See also the numerical example presented in section 5.3. and the illustrative exercise of chapter 7.)

4.5. EFFECTS OF PRICE RESTRICTIONS

Price restrictions are much less difficult to deal with when it comes to solving the problem, after allowance has been made for them and when assessing the effect they have on solution values. Also they can rather easily be introduced: if financial limitations are responsible for restrictions of the price policy, these can be introduced explicitly so that their role is represented in the model; one may also account for price restrictions by adding appropriate upper and/or lower limits on prices in the dual formulation. The latter approach seems to be the simplest way out in cases where price rigidity is motivated by factors that cannot easily be expressed in an economic plan, such as, e.g. political factors.

The effect on solution values is rather obvious: as the system of evaluations in the solution is allowed to differ only to a limited degree from the actual system, the activity levels are forced to remain within a closer range to the actual values than would have been the case without the restrictions.

51

This follows, of course, from the very nature of a more restrictive formulation.

This consideration implies further that the value of the objective function in the optimum is *unfavourably* affected, because the area of permissible solution values has been reduced. Admittedly, this effect will occur only if the price restrictions are active, *i.e.* if they do indeed restrict the feasible area. But this is highly likely, at least in the first stage, because the price restrictions have to be introduced precisely in order to avoid too wide a deviation from the market prices. Further, considering that the solution values form an interrelated system, it implies clearly that the entire solution, including the quantity (primal) solution, is affected, if some of the dual prices are forced to assume different values.

The insertion of price constraints has also important implications for the formulation of the primal problem. Normally, restrictions expressing ranges of still-acceptable values are confined to the primal – e.g. highest acceptable level of unemployment or deficit on the balance of payments – where the prices in the dual solution are left free to settle at levels that conform with these requirements. So if now the dual formulation includes such acceptability constraints, the problem is turned inside out and the variables in the primal formulation have now to be left free, or else two related constraints, say, the maximum permissable level of unemployment and the minimum wage rate, may appear to be incompatible. Thus if the emphasis devoted to the other side of the problem is increased, a shift in emphasis at the expense of the primal formulation is, in fact, achieved (see also section 7.4.).

There is another important point of a practical nature which has to do with the difficulty of obtaining the required elasticities for the augmented problem. For the immediate effect of price restrictions is to limit deviations from the actual prices, so application of the available elasticities will still be acceptable. If, however, dual prices had been allowed to differ grossly from prices observed in reality, these elasticities might *no longer be applicable* and it might be very hard and perhaps even impossible to estimate alternative elasticities pertaining to the equilibrium prices, if the latter did indeed assume extreme values. Estimates of parameters relating to extreme situations may be very hazardous, if the only source of reference is a statistical test based on 'normal' (actual) observations. Thus, price restrictions help to avoid, or, at least, reduce this complication, without which the statistical load is heavy enough.

A still more drastic simplification is obtained if significant price variations are virtually excluded. In that case *no price changes* will be allowed to occur and, thus, no price elasticities will be needed for the items involved. Other variables which depend on the prices of such items will now remain unaffected, so the special calculation procedure to be applied in order to find the equilibrium will be redundant.

The question remains whether prices which are effectively limited in range by price restrictions (excluding the non-negativity condition) can still be called shadow prices, even if they have been derived under due consideration of the equilibrium conditions discussed in chapter 2. One can also debate whether prices, which are themselves unrestricted, but which have undergone the influence of limitations on other prices, can truly be considered as shadow prices. And yet it can be argued that those prices which have reached their limits can still be included among shadow prices if only they are relatively close to their equilibrium value. But these are minor terminological questions which can simply be solved by letting the term shadow prices apply only to those prices which are in equilibrium (clear the market) *and* which remain within the price bounds. If they are effectively bounded, but significantly different from the corresponding market prices, they could be called restricted shadow prices.

As regards the effect of the equilibrium aspect on the role of price constraints in planning models, the tentative conclusion formulated in the preceding section appears to be of some help. It will be recalled that if certain conditions are satisfied – mainly requiring dominating direct effects from price changes – the equilibrium price will be closer to the price level observed in reality than the dual price derived in the solution of the planning problem applying linear programming, which ignores the equilibrium. Therefore, under these conditions and programming for equilibrium, the price restrictions, which are introduced precisely in order to limit the movement away from actual prices, may well tend to be less restrictive and may even become inactive.

4.6. SUMMARY OF THE DISCUSSION

Many of the concepts and problems discussed so far are rooted in branches of the economic discipline with which practitioners of development planning are only rarely familiar. For this reason, the following summary may be useful, since it brings together the main problems and concepts, their interrelations and consequences as they have been presented above. In a few instances reference has already been made to subsequent chapters in order to indicate the subjects to be dealt with below in relation to those discussed already.

Schematic summary of concepts, interrelations, problems and consequences discussed in the text (figures between brackets indicate the relevant chapters and sections)

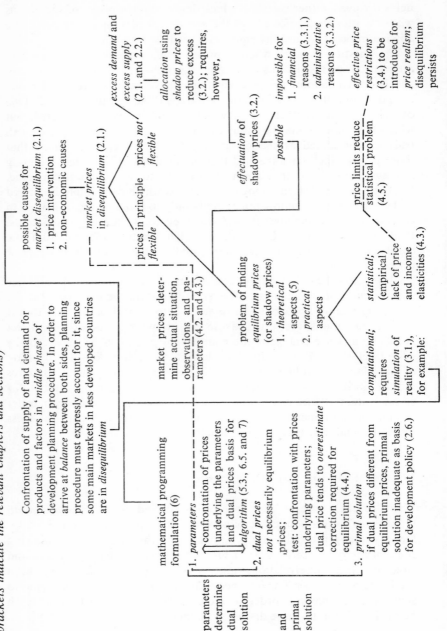

5. The equilibrium concept in economic models

5.1. SOME TYPES OF EQUILIBRIUM

The concept of equilibrium is one of the pivots around which this study revolves, which is why it deserves some special attention. Nevertheless, this chapter will deal with it in a rather superficial way as far as some aspects are concerned that do not bear much importance for the main theme of this book. The reader interested in a more profound treatment is referred to the literature[1]. Only when a direct link exists with the subject matter of this book, will our discussion go into more detail, such as in section 5.4., where some equilibrium conditions are examined that are directly related to a solution procedure for a consistent programming formulation to be presented in chapter 6. Section 5.2. contains some remarks on the relation between the optimum and the equilibrium, whereas the numerical example presented in 5.3 may help to clarify the nature of some of the problems involved.

According to F. MACHLUP's definition[2], an *equilibrium* is a constellation of selected interrelated variables so adjusted to one another that no inherent tendency to change prevails in the model in which they occur. Such a situation implies, therefore, that the variables in which the equilibrium has been expressed have settled down at a position of rest; there is no more movement originating from the system itself. When considering this, one may start to wonder what the practical significance of equilibrium really is in a world where everything changes. In economics, apparently, equilibrium will rarely exist, a situation of disequilibrium is far more likely to occur than the stationary state. Indeed the practical

---

1. For an introductory analysis R. DORFMAN, 1964, or R. H. LEFTWICH, 1966, may be recommended. For a somewhat more rigorous treatment see e.g. R. G. D. ALLEN, 1964, and A. C. CHIANG, 1967, and for a penetrating discussion and further references M. MORISHIMA, 1964, and P. A. SAMUELSON, 1947. T. NEGISHI, 1962, presents a convenient survey article. An advanced and comprehensive presentation can be found in R. E. KUENNE, 1963.
2. F. MACHLUP, 1958.

value of equilibrium analysis derives from the fact that it can be considered as a starting point for a better understanding of what may happen in a situation of disequilibrium and why, and which are the conditions that have to be fulfilled in order that the extent of the disequilibrium will grow smaller.

This brings us to the *stability* of equilibrium, which is concerned with the property that a deviation from the equilibrium sets in motion a process that will ultimately lead to a return to equilibrium. For practical purposes, one is clearly only interested in stable equilibrium, for a balanced situation, which is only reached by accident and does not act as a centre of gravity after subsequent deviations have taken place, is of little value in a continuously changing world. The process through which stable equilibrium is reached is then typically the dynamic part of the analysis of equilibrium.

Thus, if equilibrium is stable, it is a valuable concept in economic applications, indicating the locus around which the variables involved may move. Although reality will always deviate from it, it helps to know how the 'average' pattern will look: the equilibrium position is a point of orientation and the random deviations are the 'noise' that cannot be avoided in the real world. In some isolated cases such a stable equilibrium may be a useful guide for a relatively long time, namely if the deviations are continuously of a random nature. But in the majority of cases the changes will follow a certain tendency: there is growth, development, creeping inflation, changes in taste, etc. It must be emphasized, though, that a situation of equilibrium does *not* necessarily require that *all* variables remain unchanged. This condition is to be satisfied only by the variable(s) in which the equilibrium has been expressed; in this respect, the alterations of other variables are of no importance. Therefore, one equilibrium may be much more persistent than another, although, eventually, every equilibrium situation is bound to be disrupted. A new equilibrium may take its place, until it is, in turn, overthrown, and so on. Thus, as an approximation, the process of change can be regarded as a chain of equilibria, each succeeding the other more or less quickly according to the need for precision and the variability of the relevant magnitudes.

The study of the moving equilibria is the subject of *comparative statics* where only the equilibrium situations are examined and compared, but in which the transitional movements between the equilibria are neglected. The comparative-statics approach can only be applied effectively to simple models, because it requires that equilibrium points be determined directly. For example, it is easy to find the equilibrating price-quantity point (if it exists) in an isolated market with the supply and demand

56

functions given. And if this equilibrium is disrupted, the next one can equally simply be determined if the new functions are known. However, with multiple, interrelated markets, side restrictions and non-linear functions, equilibrium points are much more difficult to ascertain and the most efficient procedure may well be to *simulate the dynamic process* that leads from the original point to the new equilibrium. Even then, the two equilibrium situations can be analysed of course, but the comparison of these static positions is a separate chapter in an essentially dynamic process.

In development planning we are concerned with the entire economy, so the type of equilibrium relevant in this framework is the *general equilibrium* which involves the multitude of markets that together constitute a nation's economy. The multiplicity of markets is an essential characteristic of the general equilibrium, so the term is not applicable to a macro-model that does not distinguish between markets. On the other hand, the market equilibrium is confined to one market only – assuming that adjustments in one market can be isolated from other markets. The term partial equilibrium might be reserved for the equilibrium that takes into account the interrelations between a number of markets – together only making up a part of the economy – without links with outside markets. But many authors use the terms market and partial equilibrium alternatively to describe all equilibrium situations covering less than the general equilibrium.

5.2. OPTIMUM AND EQUILIBRIUM

The way in which the concept of equilibrium has been introduced in the foregoing chapters may have left the impression that it is a desirable situation *per se*. As there are different shades of desirability of an equilibrium, a few qualifying remarks are appropriate. First, an equilibrium situation is, indeed, preferable to one of disequilibrium, all other things being equal. Instability in itself serves no purpose; variations and fluctuations are only desirable in as far as they lead to a state superior to the one that existed before the change[3].

But the equilibrium does *not necessarily coincide* with an optimum and only the latter is worth aiming at. The classic example of an equilibrium that is less than optimal is provided by the Keynesian model of an equilibrium level of national income without full employment. (Here, equilibrium does not refer, of course, to the price-quantity equilibrium, as it

3. See J. R. HICKS, 1946, chapter 10.

did above.) But the Walrasian general equilibrium situation with which we are concerned here is not desirable in itself either, except for the fact that it may be better than an unbalanced situation. An equilibrium becomes truly desirable only if it is linked to the achievement of an objective, such as, for example, the maximum-profit production programme of a firm. In that case there is no more tendency to change as far as the firm is concerned, when this point is reached, for the very reason that it is its optimum. Such an equilibrium may be called a *goal equilibrium*.

Although the two are not necessarily the same, an optimum, on the other hand, is only really *meaningful* if it is a stable equilibrium as well. Otherwise, of course, there would be a persistent tendency away from the optimum, and under such circumstances it would be useless to even try to reach that situation. In fact, if there were no possibility of coincidence between optimum and equilibrium, this would be a blow to the economic discipline: being typically concerned with optima, it would lose a lot of its attraction if such situations were not practically feasible.

Fortunately, we know that optima do exist which are at the same time equilibrium points – the case has been mentioned already of the profit-maximizing firm, fixing production at the point where the marginal cost curve intersects the marginal revenue curve upward from the left (with 'quantity' on the vertical axis, and 'price' on the horizontal axis). The latter addition has to be made since a marginal cost curve intersecting the marginal revenue curve upward from the right implies increasing profitability with growing production, which keeps the firm from settling down at a certain production schedule. Therefore, for an equilibrium to occur under a certain preference function (say, maximizing profit), *appropriate conditions* (in this case: regarding the slopes of the marginal revenue and the marginal cost curves) must be fulfilled. It could even be argued that an optimum, by its very nature, will logically tend to be a point of convergence under an optimizing behaviour, although it must be added that a number of factors complicate this simple picture drastically[4].

Another example of the happy coincidence of equilibrium and optimum can be obtained from the theory of welfare economics which showed that in the theoretical model of universal perfect competition the equilibrium situation would also optimize welfare. This is why, in this context, we have used the term equilibrium prices as being something favourable. Similarly, shadow prices are the equilibrium prices that go hand in hand with an optimal situation which is believed to be attainable in practice.

4. For a further discussion which lies beyond the scope of this book, see G. DEBREU, 1959, chapters 5 and 6.

5.3. A NUMERICAL EXAMPLE

5.3.1. An inventor's dilemma

In our discussion so far we have projected the concept of price consistency against the background of an unspecified national development plan. In point of fact, the concept is also applicable to other fields of applied economics, which will be illustrated by the numerical example presented in this section. Yet the main reason for choosing the example from a different sphere is not to demonstrate the universality of the subject, but rather to avoid at this stage the elaborate investigations and calculations that a real planning problem would entail. The degree of realism of the model need not bother us yet and a very simple illustrative exercise will probably reveal more about the nature of the problem and its consequences than a more cumbersome analysis. So let us exchange the planning bureau temporarily for the workshop of an inventor who is gradually coming to the conclusion that economic problems start when technical difficulties have been solved.

The process this inventor has developed allows production of two fertilizer products (Evergreen and Overgrown) in fixed combinations which differ with the inputs, and where the inputs are four different by-products of other production processes. When he starts to explore the market for his products he soon finds that the volumes he can expect to sell depend inversely on the prices charged for the products, and with some effort he determines the demand curves. Further, after having acquired the necessary information, he is able to draft the supply curves of the inputs. In addition to this the technical coefficients of the production process, *i.e.* the amount of fertilizer that can be produced with the four inputs are, of course, also known. He has also calculated the other costs per unit of input, such as the cost of transporting the inputs into the factory, labour and capital costs involved in production and he adds a profit margin that can be considered a reasonable reward for his efforts.

His policy will be to content himself with this 'entrepreneurial wage' and to make prices as low as possible in order to discourage potential competitors. Thus, prices have to be made equal to average costs per unit, thereby reducing possible extra-profits to zero[5]. Finally, average

5. This may seem to be somewhat peculiar behaviour for an entrepreneur; one would rather expect him to maximize profits. Such an attitude would have required the equalization of marginal costs and marginal revenues which could have been easily arranged by a slight reformulation of the model; there is no technical difficulty here. But, unfortunately it would have disrupted the direct correspondence between

costs per unit of output are to be minimized. This information has been presented schematically below:

Outputs \ Inputs	A	B	C	D	Sales
Evergreen	.13	.15	.20	.40	q_e
Overgrown	.55	.45	.37	.15	q_0
Costs	c_A	c_B	c_C	c_D	

where q_e (the sales volume of Evergreen) decreases as p_e (the price of Evergreen) rises:

$$q_e = 9,600 - 500\, p_e, \tag{5.1}$$

where a similar relation exists between q_0 (sales of Overgrown) and p_0 (price of Overgrown):

$$q_0 = 8,060 - 300\, p_0, \tag{5.2}$$

and where the cost coefficients of inputs A, B, C and D (in \$ per unit of input) are composed as follows (note that the prices of inputs rise with the quantities bought):

	Transport, labour and capital costs	Profit margin	Price of inputs (≥ 0)
c_A	6.5	1.0	$1/2,500\, q_A - 2.8$
c_B	6.2	1.0	$1/3,000\, q_B - .8$
c_C	6.0	1.0	$1/2,500\, q_C - 2.4$
c_D	5.5	1.0	$1/4,000\, q_D - 1.0$

actual, or assumed prices (the 'in-prices' below) and the dual prices (the 'out-prices') that we find in macro-models. The present price policy conforms with the usual treatment of profits in the input-output part of multi-sector models, namely as constant proportions of the value of output. The procedure developed here for a micro-economic problem therefore becomes immediately comparable with the multi-sector case.

The inventor's dilemma will now be clear: how can he fix the production programme if *sales* depend on the *prices* he will charge, where prices depend upon the *costs per unit*, which vary in turn with the *quantities* he will *put in*, whilst the latter can only be derived if he knows the amounts of Evergreen and Overgrown he can *sell*? In an undeterminate situation like this, the problem he faces is not an easy one to solve, for if prices are fixed arbitrarily, who guarantees that the mechanism described above will not result in such high cost coefficients that he will lose on every product sold? He would have to increase his prices and reduce sales and, as a consequence, input volumes and input prices until his losses were cancelled. On the other hand, if prices were high compared with costs, he would have to lower his prices and sell more until his extra-profits have dwindled to zero.

Rather than hoping for the best and trying to find the equilibrium through a series of adaptations in actual transactions, with unforeseen and perhaps nasty consequences, the inventor decides to search for it in simulating reality. The reasoning developed in the foregoing paragraph has aroused in him the expectation that what seemed to be a vicious circle will appear to be an inward-turning spiral with a final solution, But in order to carry out the simulation exercise, the values of the variables in the first table must be specified. From the market survey he has learnt that prices in the order of magnitude of $13.20 for Evergreen and $10.20 for Overgrown would put him in a reasonably competitive position. He finds from (5.1.) and (5.2.) that the sales volumes corresponding to these prices are 3,000 and 5,000 units respectively. With revenues provisionally fixed in this way, the least-cost combination of inputs must now be found with which the two products can be made in the proper proportion. For this purpose one clearly needs the value of the cost coefficients, but these cannot be fixed unambiguously either at this stage, since they depend on the amounts of inputs used, which can only be determined by calculating the least-cost programme and for this, we have agreed already, one had to know the cost coefficients. In order to rid himself of this problem the inventor decides to ignore for the moment the prices he would have to pay for his inputs.

Evidently, the problem as it stands now is of the simple linear-programming type *(for initial tableau and optimal solution, see p. 62)*. It appears that the optimal programme requires inputs of 7,730 units of *A* and 4,987 units of *D* involving costs to the amount of $90,394. The table also gives the dual solution, *i.e.* the dual prices of Evergreen and Overgrown (after correction for the negative sign) in the bottom row in the columns of the artificial variables.

	Inputs				Artificial variables		
	A	B	C	D	V_1	V_2	Sales
Evergreen	.13	.15	.20	.40	1	0	3,000 (p_e = \$13.20)
Overgrown	.55	.45	.37	.15	0	1	5,000 (p_0 = \$10.20)
Costs	7.5	7.2	7.0	6.5			minimize

optimal solution[6]

	Inputs				Artificial variables		
	A	B	C	D	V_1	V_2	Sales
Evergreen	0	.120	.309	1	2.743	−.648	4,987
Overgrown	1	.785	.588	0	−.748	1.995	7,730
Costs	0	.531	.580	0	−12.220	−10.747	90,394

5.3.2. A consistent production programme

The inventor, contemplating his next moves, first observes that the prices he assumed to hold initially, differ from the costs per unit. Thus, it *seems* as if a profit of 98 ¢ would be made per unit sold of Evergreen and a loss of 55 ¢ per unit of Overgrown. But this, of course, is not true, because the cost coefficients of A and D which determine the level of the dual prices are not in accordance with the quantities of the inputs used in the process. However, this can now easily be corrected by substituting the solution values of A en D in their supply functions given above. With these newly obtained cost coefficients it is a simple job to calculate the true profit/loss per unit, at least if the A-D combination remains the optimal one. Thereafter the prices of Evergreen and Overgrown can be adjusted in the direction of the dual prices as has been argued above.

6. Calculations have been carried out to five decimal places.

These new prices result in new sales volumes and, ultimately in different cost coefficients, so another round of calculations is required, and so on.

In order to cut down the procedure the inventor decides to carry out two adjustments in one step: an adaptation of the cost coefficients in accordance with the input volumes derived in the first round and an adaptation of the prices of the two products towards the dual prices obtained earlier. When determining the extent of the latter adjustment he takes account of the unsteady nature of the dual prices which makes them a rather crude indicator – they also vary in the procedure. He decides to go only part of the way and adds to (or subtracts from) the prices assumed initially a rather arbitrary thirty per cent of the difference with the dual prices.

So in the second round the prices of Evergreen and Overgrown implicit in the problem are set at $(13.20 + .3(12.22 - 13.20) =)$ \$12.91 and $(10.20 + +.3(10.75 - 10.20) =)$ \$10.37 respectively, which correspond with sales volumes of 3,145 and 4,949 units of each of the two products. The cost coefficients of A and D are calculated by

$$c_A = 7.5 + \frac{7,730}{2,500} - 2.8 = 7.79 \quad \text{and}$$

$$c_D = 6.5 + \frac{4,987}{4,000} - 1.0 = 6.75.$$

This new problem can again be solved, whereafter examination of the solution values may require still another round of calculations, and so on, until at some point the prices put into the problem are equal to the prices coming out of it *and* the cost coefficients assumed are consistent with the required levels of input products. This iterative routine is far from exciting, so we skip this stage and move on to examine a summary of the findings.

Table 5.1. gives the pattern of assumed prices of Evergreen and Overgrown on the basis of which the sales volumes were determined (the in-prices) and the dual prices as they were calculated in the same iteration (the out-prices). The same figures have been plotted in graph 5.1. to illustrate more clearly the rather capricious course of the prices. Although the adaptation process took twenty iterations to converge – the calculations were terminated when the pairs of in- and out-prices became equal in the fifth decimal – the graph shows clearly that a fairly accurate impression could be obtained after only ten iterations.

The same conclusion can be derived from table 5.2., which gives the volumes of inputs and outputs through the calculations. In the last itera-

Table 5.1. In-prices and out-prices of the iterative procedure (in $)[a]

Iteration	Price of Evergreen		Price of Overgrown	
	in-price	out-price	in-price	out-price
1	13.200	12.220	10.200	10.747
2	12.910	12.688	10.370	11.167
3	12.840	13.036	10.610	10.939
4	12.900	13.180	10.710	10.780
5	12.980	13.165	10.730	10.764
6	13.036	13.075	10.740	10.790
7	13.045	13.021	10.755	10.814
8	13.035	13.015	10.773	10.810
9	13.029	13.032	10.784	10.797
10	13.030	13.041	10.788	10.787
11	13.033	13.042	10.788	10.782
12	13.036	13.038	10.786	10.783
13	13.036	13.034	10.785	10.786
14	13.036	13.032	10.785	10.787
15	13.035	13.034	10.786	10.786
16	13.035	13.035	10.786	10.786
17	13.035	13.035	10.786	10.785
18	13.035	13.035	10.786	10.785
19	13.035	13.035	10.786	10.785
20	13.035	13.035	10.785	10.785

a. Calculations have been carried out with increasing precision; in the last seven iterations five decimal places have been used.

tion a situation is reached where *no more adaptations are required*, since the prices of Evergreen and Overgrown ($13.04 and $10.79 respectively) are exactly equal to the average costs of producing one unit of each of these goods. At these prices, sales are 3,083 and 4,824 units – compare eqs. (5.1) and (5.2) in subsection 5.3.1. – which require inputs of the lowest cost combination of 7,318 units of *A* and 5,328 units of *D*. The prices paid for the inputs at these volumes are 12.7 ¢ and 33.2 ¢ per unit of *A* and *D* respectively – compare the cost-composition table in 5.3.1. – which imply with the other cost components in turn that the dual prices/ costs are $13.04 for Evergreen and $10.79 for Overgrown. Even though our inventor has no concern for the market equilibrium as such, it is clearly in his interest to organize his production programme in accordance

Graph 5.1. In– and out-prices through the iterations

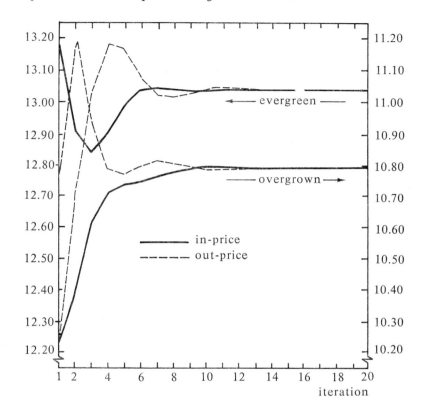

with the optimal solution because only then, and in the absence of external disturbances, will he not be bothered by market forces that compel him to change his price and production policy all the time. In addition, prices are at a minimum, since they have been made equal to average costs which have been minimized. In other words, the final solution represents an optimum *as well as* an equilibrium situation, where the optimum derives from the equality of prices and minimum average costs and where the correspondence between prices on the one hand, and quantities on the other indicates the equilibrium (recall section 5.1.). Other solutions do not possess these qualities and have therefore only a limited value.

65

Table 5.2. Volumes of inputs bought and outputs sold in the iterative procedure[a]

Iteration	Sales of products		Inputs required	
	Evergreen	Overgrown	A	D
1	3000.0	5000.0	7730.0	4987.0
2	3145.0	4949.0	7525.0	5420.0
3	3180.0	4877.0	7351.0	5552.0
4	3150.0	4847.0	7314.0	5500.0
5	3110.0	4841.0	7332.0	5393.0
6	3082.0	4838.0	7346.5	5318.5
7	3077.5	4833.5	7340.7	5309.5
8	3082.5	4828.1	7326.3	5326.7
9	3085.5	4824.8	7317.5	5337.1
10	3085.0	4823.6	7315.5	5336.5
11	3083.4	4823.7	7315.9	5330.6
12	3082.1	4824.2	7318.0	5326.7
13	3081.8	4824.5	7318.7	5325.7
14	3082.2	4824.4	7318.3	5326.7
15	3082.6	4824.3	7317.9	5327.8
16	3082.7	4824.3	7317.8	5328.1
17	3082.6	4824.3	7317.9	5328.0
18	3082.6	4824.3	7318.0	5327.8
19	3082.5	4824.3	7318.1	5327.6
20	3082.5	4824.3	7318.1	5327.6

a. Also here calculations have ultimately been carried out to two more decimal places than presented.

In concluding this subsection, it is important to observe again that the final solution – the only one which is really interesting – must fulfil certain conditions which are not easily met. It follows that it would be a remarkable coincidence if such a solution were found at once. In a textbook exercise the problem can be freely assumed to be precisely in the equilibrium situation where calculations terminate, but in problems based on reality one cannot always expect an instant equilibrium to be available. Once again, this assumption is nevertheless implicitly made when practical linear programming problems are limited to one iteration without checking whether this is justified.

5.3.3. Discussion of the results

The value of an example is of course rather limited especially when it relates to a primitive model such as the present one, which is, amongst other things, restricted to the partial equilibrium, whereas we are specially interested in the general equilibrium. Also in another sense it treats a special case as will be seen subsequently. But it may help to clarify a train of thought and may hint at matters that are of particular importance in a general treatment. In this discussion we shall concentrate on the latter aspect of the exercise.

An important observation is, of course, that the iterative procedure ends up indeed in a situation that does not require further calculations. It shows that *convergence* is possible although it leaves an even more important question unanswered, because we should like to know whether convergence can always be expected, if not, what conditions are to be fulfilled, and how do these compare with reality? Here the example cannot help us, so these questions have to be postponed until we come to a general analysis.

One striking phenomenon in our exercise is that the basis did not change in the procedure, or, in less technical language, that the combination of *A* and *D* remained the least-cost combination throughout the calculations. This is rather remarkable, because the changes in the cost row, as well as those in the column of sales volumes, might have required a different combination. The increased costs of *A* and *D* might have reduced the comparative advantage of this combination to such an extent that another one might have become a more attractive proposition. Alternatively, at some point in the procedure, Evergreen and Overgrown might have been sold in a proportion that cannot be procured by the combination of *A* and *D*.

The stability of the basis is thus to some extent the result of the moderation of the fluctuations in the sales volumes of Evergreen and Overgrown. Evergreen increased from 3,000 to 3,083 units, which is only plus 2.7 per cent with a price reduction from $13.20 to $13.04, and sales of Overgrown fell from 5,000 to 4,824 units (minus 3.5 per cent) whilst its price went up steadily to $10.79 from an initial level of $10.20. In a practical case one may have started to wonder if, after all, these results justify the effort. But all this could, of course, easily have been different; it just means that the initial assumptions were not very far off the mark. It is also very hard to foresee how the final solution will look in a more realistic and, thus, more complicated problem.

There is still the question of the *adaptation coefficient*. In the exercise it has been kept constant at thirty per cent. It seems reasonable to expect that, with a different figure, the number of iterations one would have to go through before the final destination is reached, would have been affected. But there are obvious restrictions to the value one may reasonably assume; for example, there is no ground for a negative coefficient which would adjust the in-prices away from the out-prices of the previous iteration. On the other hand, too high a coefficient would at least delay convergence as it would make the difference between two iterations more pronounced than desirable. Probably an optimal figure will exist in the sense that it will reduce the number of iterations to the minimum. A variable coefficient may well appear to be the best solution, but it remains to be seen which approach will be most efficient: to determine the optimal corrector from iteration to iteration (supposing that it were possible to find it) or to use a reasonable, fixed coefficient, without bothering too much about the length of the procedure.

The reader may have already noticed that the successive solution values do *not* approach the equilibrium values *monotonously*, even if different definitions of monotonous processes of convergence are applied. In every case it requires a continuous diminution of the distance between two vectors as the iterations proceed, but the type of vectors compared will differ with the definitions. In the terms of our example, the definition may relate to the distances between the vectors of out-prices and the vector of the ultimate equilibrium prices, or to the distances between the vectors of in-prices and out-prices in the same iteration, or to the distances between the vectors of out-prices in successive iterations. Every definition, if it is fulfilled, guarantees that an equilibrium will eventually be reached; with every step one gets closer to the final solution, not only in terms of iterations still to be carried out, since this is common to any converging process, but rather in terms of the distance that remains to be bridged.

It appears that, whichever criterion is applied, the procedure fails to converge monotonously, though the extent of the failures is fairly small as the disturbances occur only when the distances have already been strongly reduced. Further, the deviations from the monotonous pattern take place in different stages of the procedure as different criteria are applied.

5.4. STABILITY CONDITIONS AND OTHER DYNAMIC ASPECTS

In this section the stability conditions of two patterns of adaptation will be examined as an introduction to the iterative solution procedures described in chapter 6. First, the stability conditions of two dynamic models for the simplest type of equilibrium – the market equilibrium – will be treated, thereafter we derive the conditions for convergence of the adaptation pattern applied in the numerical example of the foregoing section, and finally we turn to the stability conditions of an excess-demand adaptation pattern for general equilibrium.

The derivation of the stability conditions presented below makes use of differential equations, although solution procedures are of course expressed in discrete changes. The complications resulting from this jump will be ignored, however.

5.4.1. Market equilibrium

Case I. The excess-demand approach
Of the dynamic equilibrium models proposed so far, the excess-demand approach, as it may be called, is easily the most familiar one. Its pattern of adaptation is based on the assumption that, departing from a state of initial disequilibrium, price will rise if demand exceeds supply, and price will fall if supply exceeds demand. The stability conditions of this approach follow easily.

Let the demand and supply equations be given by

$$q_D = ap + b,\tag{5.3}$$

$$q_S = cp + d,\tag{5.4}$$

where q = quantity (D for demand and S for supply)
p = price.

The equilibrium price p^0 is the one that equates demand and supply, so, if $q_D = q_S$, it follows that $p^0 = \dfrac{d-b}{a-c}$. The adaptation pattern can be expressed as $\dot{p} = \dfrac{dp}{dt} = k(q_D - q_S)$, in which k (>0) is the adaptation coefficient which translates the excess demand into the price change. Substituting (5.3) and (5.4) in this differential equation, we get

$$\dot{p} = k(ap + b - cp - d) = k\{(a-c)p - (d-b)\}.\tag{5.5}$$

Since $(d-b) = (a-c)p^0$, (5.5) may be rewritten as

$$\dot{p} = k(a-c)(p - p^0).\tag{5.6}$$

69

The solution of this differential equation indicates the time path of p through the adjustment process:

$$p(t) = p^0 + (p - p^0) e^{k(a-c)t}. \qquad (5.7)$$

From this equation it is clear that in order to converge, the second term right of the equality sign should dwindle to zero as time proceeds; only then will $p(t)$ become equal to p^0 in the end. And this situation will only be achieved if $k(a-c) < 0$, which implies, with $k > 0$, that

$$a - c < 0, \qquad (5.8)$$

which is the familiar Walrasian condition for stable equilibrium, requiring that the coefficient indicating the slope of the demand curve is smaller than that of the supply curve.

Case II. The excess-price approach[7]

As an introduction to the discussion in the next subsection, let us see what the stability conditions of the adjustment process adopted for the numerical example of section 5.3. looks like for the equilibrium in an isolated market. In this approach one starts with an arbitrary demand price (in-price) and finds the corresponding demand quantity; for the same quantity the corresponding supply price (out-price) is then determined. If the out-price is lower than the initial in-price, price is adjusted downwards; if the out-price turns out to be higher, price is increased.

Using the same symbols and relations as in the foregoing case, but slightly adapted to indicate the different direction of dependencies, we have

$$q = a p_D + b, \qquad (5.3a)$$

$$p_S = \frac{1}{c} q - \frac{d}{c}. \qquad (5.4a)$$

As this system of equations is identical to (5.3) and (5.4), the equilibrium price must, of course, be the same as before. So $p^0 = \dfrac{d-b}{a-c}$. But the

---

7. Note that the approach as it is meant here, differs from Marshall's excess-price approach. Its equilibrium conditions are, therefore, also different. See e.g. B. HANSEN, 1970, p. 14.

70

adjustment pattern is different, and becomes now

$$\dot{p}_D = h(p_S - p_D) = h\left(\frac{a-c}{c} p_D + \frac{b-d}{c}\right) =$$

$$\dot{p}_D = h\left(\frac{a-c}{c}\right)(p_D - p^0), \qquad (h > 0). \tag{5.9}$$

Thus, the time pattern for the present process of adaptation becomes

$$p_D(t) = p^0 + (p_D - p^0) e^{h\left(\frac{a-c}{c}\right)t}, \tag{5.10}$$

and it follows that a stable equilibrium requires that

$$\frac{a-c}{c} < 0, \qquad (h > 0), \tag{5.11}$$

or, expressed differently,

$$a < c, \quad \text{if} \quad c > 0,$$

$$a > c, \quad \text{if} \quad c < 0.$$

The stability conditions of the two procedures prove to be identical if $c > 0$, which is traditionally assumed to be normal. But if the supply curve slopes downwards, the conditions are opposed.

The adaptation patterns with 'normally' sloping demand and supply curves are illustrated below. The characteristic difference between the two approaches is also clearly brought out by the graphs: in the first case, excess-demand quantities are translated into price adjustments, whereas in the second case excess-prices guide the adaptation pattern.

In these dynamic models an important role is played by the *adjustment coefficients* k and h, which determine the length of the stride taken, one hopes, from a certain position towards the equilibrium. If the adaptations are infinitesimally small the value of these coefficients creates no problem as we have just seen, as long as they are only positive. But in real cases one works with *discrete changes* and then the magnitude of the adaptation coefficient has indeed an impact on the adjustment pattern and its result.

The sensitivity of the outcome of the process in relation to these coefficients can be explained more easily with the help of the graphs than in mathematical terms. It can immediately be seen from graphs 5.2a and 5.2b that with high values for k and h one may overshoot the equilibrium price. In itself, there is nothing wrong with this, since the new step will again point in the right direction if the necessary conditions are fulfilled.

But, if k and h have been chosen too high, an oscillatory movement will commence, moving farther and farther away from the equilibrium. In order to be completely sure about the correct value of the adaptation parameter, one should, therefore, know the equilibrium position in advance. But this would be catching a horse to catch a horse, since it is the equilibrium we want to find with the help of this parameter.

Graph 5.2. Adjustment pattern in the excess-demand and the excess-price approach

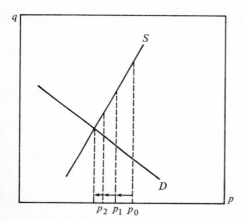 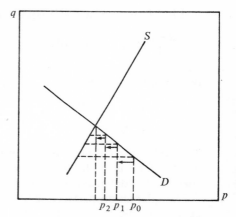

5.2a. Case I, excess-demand approach.

5.2b. Case II, excess-price approach.

The problem of the value of the parameter cannot be solved unequivocally, therefore. One can construct cases where it would be wise to make it very large, but in other cases this would be very unwise. With a rather small value one is always on the safe side, but the number of steps may thus become excessive. In this way, the value selected tends to become a matter of temperament rather than of straightforward reasoning. The best approach seems to be to keep a wary eye on the time pattern of the variables involved; if, in successive stages, the adaptations continue to point in the same direction, there is reason to increase the adaptation parameter; if they go up and down, it could be reduced, and it should be reduced if the oscillations grow wider and wider.

5.4.2. Partial equilibrium

Case III
Let us now examine the conditions to be fulfilled to ensure that problems like the example treated in section 5.3. have a stable equilibrium under the adaptation behaviour proposed and applied there. This problem is slightly more complicated than the one in case II, because the supply curves of Evergreen and Overgrown are *interrelated*: if one unit of *one* of the two products is sold more, this will have consequences for the quantities needed of A and D which will be reflected in the prices of the inputs. And this change in the cost structure of the inputs will affect the supply prices of *both* Evergreen and Overgrown. On the other hand, demand for the two fertilizers is independent (see (5.1) and (5.2)).

The system of equations becomes now

$$q_1 = a_1 p_{D1} + b_1, \tag{5.12}$$

$$p_{S1} = \frac{1}{u_1} q_1 + \frac{1}{u_{21}} q_2 - \frac{w_1}{u_1}, \tag{5.13}$$

$$q_2 = a_2 p_{D2} + b_2, \tag{5.14}$$

$$p_{S2} = \frac{1}{u_2} q_2 + \frac{1}{u_{12}} q_1 - \frac{w_2}{u_2}. \tag{5.15}$$

At every step the inventor assumed certain prices for Evergreen and Overgrown, so as to determine demand for these products. Thereafter he calculated the amounts of inputs which allowed him to find the prices at which he could have offered his goods *under the circumstances dictated by the assumed prices*. He adjusted his assumed prices by a fixed proportion in the direction of the supply prices. So

$$\dot{p}_{D1} = s(p_{S1} - p_{D1}) =$$

$$= s \left\{ \frac{1}{u_1} (a_1 p_{D1} + b_1) + \frac{1}{u_{21}} (a_2 p_{D2} + b_2) - \frac{w_1}{u_1} - p_{D1} \right\} =$$

$$= s \left(\frac{a_1 - u_1}{u_1} p_{D1} + \frac{a_2}{u_{21}} p_{D2} + \frac{b_1 - w_1}{u_1} + \frac{b_2}{u_{21}} \right), \quad (s > 0), \tag{5.16}$$

$$\dot{p}_{D2} = s(p_{S2} - p_{D2}) =$$

$$= s\left\{\frac{1}{u_2}(a_2 p_{D2} + b_2) + \frac{1}{u_{12}}(a_1 p_{D1} + b_1) - \frac{w_2}{u_2} - p_{D2}\right\} =$$

$$= s\left(\frac{a_2 - u_2}{u_2} p_{D2} + \frac{a_1}{u_{12}} p_{D1} + \frac{b_2 - w_2}{u_2} + \frac{b_1}{u_{12}}\right), \quad (s > 0). \quad (5.17)$$

It is convenient to define coefficients z_{11}, z_{12}, z_{21}, z_{22}, x_1 and x_2, such that (5.16) and (5.17) are equivalent to

$$\dot{p}_{D1} = z_{11} p_{D1} + z_{21} p_{D2} + x_1, \qquad (5.16a)$$

$$\dot{p}_{D2} = z_{12} p_{D1} + z_{22} p_{D2} + x_2. \qquad (5.17a)$$

Adopting trial solutions $p_{D1} = m_1 e^{rt}$ and $p_{D2} = m_2 e^{rt}$, implying $\dot{p}_{D1} = rm_1 e^{rt}$ and $\dot{p}_{D2} = rm_2 e^{rt}$, and employing matrix notation[8], the homogeneous part of (5.16a) and (5.17a) can be written as

$$I\begin{bmatrix} m_1 \\ m_2 \end{bmatrix} re^{rt} - Z\begin{bmatrix} m_1 \\ m_2 \end{bmatrix} e^{rt} = o, \text{ which requires that } (rI - Z)\begin{bmatrix} m_1 \\ m_2 \end{bmatrix} = o.$$

$$(5.18)$$

Meaningful solutions for m_1 and m_2 can only be obtained if the determinant $|rI - Z| = 0$, that is, if

$$r^2 - (z_{11} + z_{22})r + z_{11} z_{22} - z_{12} z_{21} = 0. \qquad (5.19)$$

Similarly to the requirements in 5.4.1., the dynamic process will converge only if the exponents in the trial solutions are negative. Thus the roots of characteristic equation (5.19) must be negative:

$$r_{1,2} = \frac{(z_{11} + z_{22}) \pm \sqrt{(z_{11} - z_{22})^2 + 4 z_{12} z_{21}}}{2} < 0. \qquad (5.20)$$

As the numerical example did indeed reach a stable equilibrium, it apparently satisfied this condition, which can easily be verified. From the description of the interrelation between the supply curves of Evergreen

---

8. Throughout this book the following symbols will be used: small Latin letters indicate scalars, e.g. the parameter a_1 and the variable p_{D1}; small Greek letters are reserved for vectors, where row vectors are indicated by a transposition sign; capital Latin letters denote matrices.

and Overgrown in the first paragraph of this subsection, it follows that u_1, u_2, u_{12} and u_{21} can be obtained from

$$
\begin{bmatrix} \dfrac{1}{u_1} \\[2ex] \dfrac{1}{u_{12}} \end{bmatrix} = B^{-1} \begin{bmatrix} \dfrac{dp_D}{dq_D} & 0 \\[2ex] 0 & \dfrac{dp_A}{dq_A} \end{bmatrix} B^{-1} \begin{bmatrix} 1 \\[2ex] 0 \end{bmatrix} = \begin{bmatrix} .002100 \\[2ex] -.001115 \end{bmatrix}, \text{ and}
$$

$$
\begin{bmatrix} \dfrac{1}{u_{21}} \\[2ex] \dfrac{1}{u_2} \end{bmatrix} = B^{-1} \begin{bmatrix} \dfrac{dp_D}{dq_D} & 0 \\[2ex] 0 & \dfrac{dp_A}{dq_A} \end{bmatrix} B^{-1} \begin{bmatrix} 0 \\[2ex] 1 \end{bmatrix} = \begin{bmatrix} -.001162 \\[2ex] .001713 \end{bmatrix}, \tag{5.21}
$$

where subindices 1 and 2 stand for Evergreen and Overgrown respectively, and where B is the matrix of input coefficients of D and A. Substituting these values in (5.20) and recalling that $a_1 = -500$ and $a_2 = -300$, we find that $r_1 = -2.53s$ and $r_2 = -4.60s$ where $s > 0$, so convergence is indeed warranted.

Of course, the numerical example was not only intended to find the equilibrium. In fact, we could choose among a number of equilibria each involving a different combination of inputs. But the additional task was to select the optimal combination. Throughout the iterative process – which is equivalent to the dynamic procedure of adaptation to which we referred in this discussion of stability conditions – the A-D combination continued to be the optimal one. If this had not been the case, the tacit assumption of *continuous differentiability* in (5.16) and (5.17) would not have been met, because of a shift from one set of demand and supply functions to another. Therefore, the demonstration in the foregoing paragraph that the conditions for convergence are indeed satisfied is valid only by virtue of the fact that the basis did not change.

5.4.3. General equilibrium

Case IV
Interdependences between markets arise from various causes: products may be substitutes for each other, they may be complementary products, there may be a direct or indirect link via the production structure, a change in one market may make itself felt in other markets as a result of the income effect, etc. Some of these links will be made explicit and various

types of markets will be distinguished in our discussion below. Specifically, the input-output interdependences will be introduced separately, beside other links, whereas a distinction will be made between goods and primary factors. The LEONTIEF model, being directly derived from WALRAS' general equilibrium system, fits very easily into the discussion and also helps to bring out the relation with multi-sector planning models more clearly. The separate treatment of factors and products follows the WALRAS-LEONTIEF tradition; its function will become clear subsequently.

The presentation of the model below follows the lines set out by M. MORISHIMA[9]. Only one difference has been introduced here, namely when it comes to the adaptation pattern, which has been slightly reformulated to make it directly comparable to one of the gradient methods for equilibrium programming to be discussed in chapter 6. However, it will appear that this alteration does not affect the stability conditions.

First we have the familiar input-output relations

$$x_i = \sum_j a_{ij} x_j + g_i(p_j, v_{\hat{h}}), \qquad (i, j = 1, ..., m; \hat{h} = 1, ..., k+1), \quad (5.22a)$$

where x_i = production of product i ($i = 1, ..., m$)
$\quad a_{ij}$ = input coefficient from sector i to sector j
$\quad g_i$ = final demand for product i
$\quad p_j$ = price of product j ($j = 1, ..., m$)
$\quad v_{\hat{h}}$ = price of factor $\hat{h}$ ($\hat{h} = 1, ..., k+1$).

It will be noticed that the volumes of final demand have been made dependent on the prices of all factors and products. In matrix notation

$$\xi = A\xi + \gamma(\pi, \delta), \qquad (5.22b)$$

where the symbols have been employed as indicated above (in most cases the Greek symbol adopted for a vector is the analogon of the Latin symbol for its elements, e.g. $\xi = \langle x_1 . .... x_m \rangle$).

Demand and supply of the primary factors are given by

$$\sum_j b_{\hat{h}j} x_j = r_{\hat{h}}(p_j, v_{\hat{h}}), \qquad (j = 1. .... m; \hat{h} = 1. .... k+1) \qquad (5.23a)$$

where $b_{\hat{h}j}$ = input coefficient of factor $\hat{h}$ into sector j
$\quad r_{\hat{h}}$ = supply of factor $\hat{h}$.

---

9. *Ibid.*, chapter 2.

Or, alternatively,

$$\hat{B}\xi = \hat{\rho}(\pi, \eth).$$ (5.23b)

The next set of relations expresses the equality of prices of products and the costs of producing them, where a distinction is made between intermediate inputs and primary inputs. Thus

$$p_j = \sum_i a_{ij} p_i + \sum_{\hat{h}} b_{\hat{h}j} v_{\hat{h}}, \qquad (i, j = 1, ..., m; \hat{h} = 1, ..., k+1)$$ (5.24a)

or

$$\pi' = \pi' A + \eth' \hat{B}.$$ (5.24b)

It can be proved that under certain conditions which are generally assumed to be fulfilled, system (5.22) up to and including (5.24) has at least one positive solution (ξ, π and $\eth > 0$) with one of the prices of primary factors (the *numéraire*) equal to unity. One of these conditions (see M. MORISHIMA, *ibid.*, p. 26) seems to be particularly stringent, namely the one which requires that functions $\gamma(\pi, \eth)$ and $\hat{\rho}(\pi, \eth)$ be *homogeneous of degree zero* in π and $\eth$. This is indeed a peculiar requirement, since there is no reason why product-demand and factor-supply functions should obey such a rule. Obviously by this we do not mean to say that these functions cannot be formulated and tested in that form. The problem only is that demand and supply functions are not naturally and exclusively homogeneous of zero degree and that a theory which nevertheless relies on such a condition does not treat more than a very particular case, the practical realism of which is doubtful.

This observation suggests a fundamental weakness of the theory of the general equilibrium. The problems which it must deal with are so complicated that very drastic assumptions must be made in order to arrive still at conclusions. Without such assumptions the problems cannot be solved, but, at the same time, they weaken the value of the outcome. With our present knowledge we can only hope – but not be sure – that the insight to be gained from a complete theory outweighs the disadvantage of its limitations.

Continuing again the discussion of stability conditions, we enter now into another crucial stage. First, let the *numéraire* be the $k+1$st factor and let us introduce new symbols v and ρ for the vectors of prices and supply volumes of primary factors respectively, excluding the $k+1$st factor. We can now define a *Jacobian matrix* J with as elements the partial derivatives of the g_i ($i = 1, ..., m$) with respect to the p_j ($j = 1, ..., m$) and the v_h ($h = 1, ..., k$) and the negative partial derivatives of the

r_h with respect to the p_j and the v_h, as follows

$$
J = \left[
\begin{array}{c|c}
\dfrac{\partial \gamma(\pi, v)}{\partial \pi} & \dfrac{\partial \gamma(\pi, v)}{\partial v} \\
\hline
-\dfrac{\partial \rho(\pi, v)}{\partial \pi} & -\dfrac{\partial \rho(\pi, v)}{\partial v}
\end{array}
\right].
$$

It is clear that the elements of J express the relation between price changes and the resulting quantity changes and they may, therefore, be compared with coefficients a, b, c, u and w in the above subsections. The latter, it will be recalled, had to satisfy certain conditions in order to reach a stable equilibrium, so one will expect that a similar role will be played here by the elements in J. In fact, here it will be required that the *quadratic form* $\lambda' J \lambda$ *be negative* for all vectors λ different from the zero vector and for non-negative prices of products and factors.

Let us examine what this rather abstract requirement implies. It is well known that the impact of a price change can be broken down into an *income* and a *substitution effect*. The income effect results from the change in real income caused by the price change, whereas the substitution effect reflects the change in the purchasing pattern purely induced by the price change that would materialize if the income change were just compensated. The same distinction between income and substitution effects applies to the reaction of supply of factors of production to a price change. Thus, matrix J can be regarded as the sum of two other matrices, one containing the income effects and the other the substitution effects.

The substitution effects in a price-induced change of demand for competitive products show a clear and simple pattern: it can rather easily be demonstrated that the substitution effect of a change in the price of a product is *negative* relative to the quantity purchased of that product, but *positive* relative to quantities of other products (substitution away from the price increase, or towards the price decrease). This is the spending side; it will not be surprising that the income-earning side displays reverse behaviour: if the price of a factor changes, the substitution effect relative to the amount of that factor offered is *positive*, whereas it is *negative* relative to the supply of other factors (substitution is directed here towards the price increase and away from the price decrease). In consequence, the matrix of substitution effects among competitive products has negative elements on its main diagonal and positive elements elsewhere (the substitution effects in the lower part of the matrix are reversed in sign in accordance with J).

78

By a classical theorem $\lambda' J\lambda$ is negative – or, in other words, J is negative definite – if all principal minors in J alternate in sign. At first sight this may seem to be a stringent condition, but it can easily be seen that a matrix of substitution effects such as this would just meet this condition. But also for the general case it can be proved – although this will not be done here[10] – that the matrix of substitution effects is negative definite.

The income effects, on the other hand, cannot be classified unambiguously; one is tempted to reason that most of the income effects relating to demand for products will be negative, but this does not bring us far enough. Guesses are even more difficult when referring to the supply of factors where rather curious patterns may occur[11].

So, if the income effects can be neglected $\lambda' J\lambda$ is indeed negative. If they are significantly different from zero, however, the condition will be still fulfilled if the substitution effects dominate, either because the income effects reinforce the substitution effects, or because they are too small to outweigh the substitution effects. J.R. HICKS[12] estimates that this is not a severe requirement. Indeed, it is generally assumed that normal market behaviour follows a pattern that reflects 'dominating' substitution effects. In graphical terms this implies demand curves sloping downwards and supply curves sloping upwards to the right, as can easily be shown. It will be recalled that very similar requirements have been derived for the simple cases examined earlier in this section.

If J possesses the above-mentioned properties, it can be shown that[13]

$$(\pi_2 - \pi_1)'(\gamma(\pi_2, v_2, 1) - \gamma(\pi_1, v_1, 1)) -$$
$$-(v_2 - v_1)'(\rho(\pi_2, v_2, 1) - \rho(\pi_1, v_1, 1)) < 0, \qquad (5.25)$$

where vectors (π_1, v_1) and (π_2, v_2) are different from each other. Inequality (5.25) expresses that for two different price vectors and their corresponding vectors of final demand and factor supply, if a price of a product in the first vector is higher than in the second, demand for that product corresponding with the first vector will fall short of the level of demand corresponding with the second, and inversely; on the other hand, if the price of a factor in one vector exceeds the price of the same factor in the

10. J.R. HICKS, *ibid.*, p. 310 *et seq.*
11. See for example M.P. TODARO, 1969, and M.P. MIRACLE and B. FETTER, 1970, on the backward sloping labour-supply curve.
12. *Ibid.*, p. 72
13. See M. MORISHIMA, *ibid.*, p. 28, for an elegant proof.

other vector, supply corresponding with the first vector will be higher than supply corresponding with the second.

It may seem that individual products or factors can deviate from this pattern, since according to (5.25) only the sum of the scalar products will be negative. But a more careful consideration shows that this is not true for the general case and that indeed all items must behave as has been described above. For, if one item behaved in an opposite fashion, its weight could be increased to such an extent that (5.25) would no longer hold. On the other hand, for *practical* purposes it is sufficient if the main factors and products behave so as to comply with (5.25). This result will be used in the proof below.

The *adaptation behaviour* in a situation of disequilibrium proposed below differs from MORISHIMA's, but the derivation of the stability conditions is similar. The present procedure is the following: if demand for factor h ($h = 1, ..., k$) exceeds (or falls short of) supply, the price of that factor is increased (or decreased). From the new vector of factor prices, the prices of the products $1, ..., m$ can be determined unambiguously, for from (5.24) it follows that

$$\pi' = v'B(I-A)^{-1} + \beta'_{k+1}(I-A)^{-1},$$ (5.26)

where B is the matrix containing the first k rows of $\hat{B}$ and where β'_{k+1} is the last row of $\hat{B}$.

With all prices given, final demand and supply of factors can now be derived. This permits us to calculate the levels of production needed to satisfy final demand, since from (5.22) we have that

$$\xi = (I-A)^{-1}\gamma(\pi, v, 1).$$ (5.27)

Hence, in this system the production volumes are always consistent with the product and factor prices. Finally, with the help of the production volumes, demand for factors can easily be determined from

$$B\xi = \rho.$$ (5.28)

A comparison of factor demand with factor supply found earlier provides the information by which a new vector of factor prices can be compiled for a new round of calculations. In symbols

$$K\dot{v} = B\xi - \rho(\pi, v, 1),$$ (5.29)

where K is a diagonal matrix with positive adaptation coefficients as

80

diagonal elements, and $\dot{v}$ is the vector of derivatives of factor prices with respect to time[14].

In the proof that this system leads to a *stable equilibrium* if $\lambda' J\lambda < 0$, we make use of the property that only in the equilibrium we have

$$B\xi^0 - \rho^0(\pi^0, v^0, 1) = B(I-A)^{-1}\gamma^0(\pi^0, v^0, 1) - \rho^0(\pi^0, v^0, 1) = 0,$$

(5.30)

where the upper index o refers to the equilibrium situation as before. So substituting (5.27) in (5.29) and using (5.30), we may write

$$K\dot{v} = B(I-A)^{-1}(\gamma(\pi, v, 1) - \gamma^0(\pi^0, v^0, 1)) -$$
$$-(\rho(\pi, v, 1) - \rho^0(\pi^0, v^0, 1)).$$

(5.31)

Now define $2y = (v - v^0)'K(v - v^0)$. This is a quadratic form, and, with diagonal elements in $K > 0$, $y \geq 0$, with strict inequality if $v \neq v^0$. Taking the derivative of y with respect to time and making use of (5.31), we get

$$\frac{dy}{dt} = (v - v^0)'K\dot{v} =$$
$$= (v - v^0)'B(I-A)^{-1}(\gamma(\pi, v, 1) - \gamma^0(\pi^0, v^0, 1)) -$$
$$-(v - v^0)'(\rho(\pi, v, 1) - \rho^0(\pi^0, v^0, 1)).$$

(5.32)

From (5.26) it can be derived that

$$(v - v^0)'B(I-A)^{-1} = (\pi - \pi^0)'.$$

(5.33)

Substituting this result in (5.32) and taking into account (5.25), it follows that

$$\frac{dy}{dt} = (\pi - \pi^0)'(\gamma(\pi, v, 1) - \gamma^0(\pi^0, v^0, 1)) -$$
$$-(v - v^0)'(\rho(\pi, v, 1) - \rho^0(\pi^0, v^0, 1)) \leq 0,$$

(5.34)

where $\dfrac{dy}{dt} = 0$, if $v = v^0$.

---

14. So this procedure operates through adaptations in the factor prices only, bypassing other possible corrections. MORISHIMA, however, assumes a threefold adaptation in each iteration, namely in product prices (in line with the corresponding excess demands), in factor prices (same) and in outputs of products (in line with profits), respectively. So the first method is more concise, but the second is probably closer to actual adaptation behaviour in market economies.

Hence, starting from an initial positive value, y continues to decrease as long as $v \neq v^0$. But it cannot fall below zero. Clearly, therefore, y approaches a value of zero, and when $y = 0$, then also $v = v^0$ and $\dot{v} = 0$. So the factor prices (and, with them, all other prices and quantities) approach their equilibrium values, and as soon as they have become equal, the adaptation process comes to a halt.

5.4.4. Concluding remarks

In this section we have examined the *conditions* required for a stable equilibrium, a. assuming different adaptation patterns, and, b. allowing for increasingly complex market structures. The principal purpose of this was, of course, to learn more about the equilibrium aspect of the price-consistency problem when price-quantity relations are explicitly taken into account. Indeed, the main findings relating to the general equilibrium problem will be used extensively in the next chapter.

But the discussion was not only meant to prepare the ground for the subsequent pages; a brief evaluation of the theory itself will be in order. In particular it seems worth while to conclude this section with some general observations regarding the nature of the assumptions that had to be made in the derivation of the conditions for stable general equilibrium, and the relation between the theoretical stability conditions and the circumstances prevailing in reality in developing countries.

It has been shown that the stability conditions for price-quantity equilibrium for the adaptation patterns and market structures considered above, would, roughly speaking, be fulfilled under a 'normal market behaviour'. This term was used to indicate supply and demand behaviour when more (less) of a product or factor is offered (used) when its price rises and less (more) is offered (used) when price falls. The fact that this behaviour is called *normal* suggests that this condition, by itself, is not considered stringent. But even at this point a complication exists, for, although it seems true that the majority of markets behave 'normally', this is not the case for all markets. Nevertheless, when discussing relation (5.25) we have seen that this is what has been required. Here it could be argued that economic reality is so thoroughly complicated that theory cannot be expected to align to it entirely, so it would be an achievement if theory corresponded with a broad tendency. On the other hand, however, the conclusion has been reached under the assumption that the market behaviour of each and every traded item is normal. Without this assumption the derivation would have ended up in a vacuum.

But even if this matter could be ignored, the next question is whether the equilibrating market behaviour, which is considered normal in industrialized countries, can also be expected to prevail in less developed countries. In view of the striking disequilibria which often exist (see chapter 2), there seems to be reason for some scepticism. Although it is hard to generalize on the basis of very little factual information, it can probably still be maintained that also in developing countries the market pattern is predominantly 'normal'. But there are a few disturbing factors which operate at the same time. There is no need to go again through the arguments developed earlier; a brief summary will suffice.

There are, firstly, the type of price disequilibria which are the result of some peculiarities and even of malfunctioning of some major markets in underdeveloped economies. An example of the former is the minimum wage level: the fact that it is binding, rather than its existence in general seems characteristic for developing countries. Causes for malfunctioning of markets are the bad communications (in a wide sense), lack of entrepreneurial skill, and so on.

The other type of disequilibrium springs from price intervention as an instrument of economic policy. As an example can be mentioned the policy of keeping the price of foreign exchange artificially low. Our comment here would be that the effects arising from the price distortion itself must be considered together with the other (intended) effects, when evaluating such a measure. This can easily be corrected in principle, if the importance of the distortive effects were realized. On the other hand, the technique of evaluating these effects is a much more difficult matter.

It must be emphasized that, even if one could prove that the general market equilibrium could in principle be reached under the circumstances prevailing in developing countries, it may be desirable and even necessary to guide the process of attaining equilibrium, rather than leave it entirely to the markets themselves to find it. Such guidance and intervention is required if the spontaneous process were otherwise unnecessarily long and were to create too much uncertainty, or, more important, if the spontaneous equilibrium were not acceptable for social considerations. Intervention in the price mechanism is warranted, of course, if there are good reasons to expect that the positive aspects (e.g. in terms of social justice) will be greater than the negative consequences of the disequilibrium that may result. Our concern is that the full impact of the latter is hardly considered, with the result that the net effect will be different from – and may even be opposite to – what was actually desired.

Above we have confronted in a summary fashion the conditions relating to market behaviour derived from a theoretical analysis with the market situation in developing countries. But it is also worth while to consider the realistic value of some of the assumptions made in the process of the derivation itself. There is more reason for this than there may perhaps seem to be at first sight. For example, an important element of the multi-sector model discussed in subsection 5.4.3. was the input-output part, describing the interdependences between the various sectors. Even though the assumptions underlying the input-output structure, e.g. those concerning proportionality between inputs and outputs, are not entirely realistic, input-output analysis is by now widely used in descriptions of the functioning of an economy. Indeed, there can be no objection, as long as the input-output matrix remains an acceptable approximation of an actual situation during a certain period. However, for the present purpose we must, again, be more strict, since the assumptions mark out the area where the theory applies. The theory loses much of its practical value outside this area.

An even more pronounced example is provided by another assumption which has been discussed above, namely concerning the demand and supply functions of goods and factors, respectively, which were required to be homogeneous of degree zero. It has already been pointed out that there is no reason to expect that this assumption will be fulfilled in reality. Again this will affect the practical usefulness of the theory.

Obviously, it would be improper to conclude merely on the basis of what has just been said that the entire theory of the general economic equilibrium remains remote from the actual situation. The introductory survey presented in this chapter is of course much too narrow a basis for such a serious conclusion, not to mention even the superficial way in which this matter has been discussed in this subsection. On the other hand, our tentative, critical observations are entirely in accordance with the result of more comprehensive evaluations. Most authors agree that there is indeed a *wide gap* between the level of *abstraction of the theory* and the *complications which exist in reality*[15]. In other words, the theoretical basis of the type of equilibrium problem that we want to tackle is not particularly solid. Returning to our starting point, it means that, with our present knowledge, a firm and unambiguous answer to the question whether stability of general market equilibrium in developing countries is feasible, cannot be given.

Hence, when examining the equilibrium aspect of the price-consistency problem, it must be realized that departing from a situation of disequi-

---

15. See for example the preface to K. J. ARROW and F. H. HAHN, 1971, p. vi, where the question is raised whether 'an inquiry into an economy, apparently so abstracted from the world, is worthwhile'. See further J. KORNAI, 1971.

librium, a stable equilibrium can only be *assumed* to be really possible. Keeping this in mind, our problem then becomes to find a planning procedure which – contrary to the traditional approach – takes the existing disequilibrium explicitly into account in an attempt to reduce the disequilibrium and, thus, to improve the allocation of resources. This matter will be dealt with in the next chapter. For a fair judgement of the general equilibrium analysis, it should now also be emphasized that some of its main elements and findings will then be very useful. In fact, it will become clear that the two solution procedures to be discussed in the next chapter practically coincide with the dynamic adaptation patterns which have been examined in this section. This circumstance will not only help to recognize some of the principal features of the solution procedures and, thus, contribute to the understanding of the economic meaning of some mathematical requirements. It also reduces the remaining problem considerably.

6. Programming for equilibrium; formulation and solution

6.1. GENERAL INTRODUCTION

This chapter will first examine how the equilibrium aspect of the price-consistency problem can be incorporated in a planning (*i.e.* optimization) model and in which way it will change the nature of the model and, second, how this new problem can be solved. The latter question will occupy the greatest portion of this chapter, with a presentation of alternative solution procedures and a discussion of the qualities of each of them. For reasons explained before, our analysis will be based on the mathematical programming formulation of a development planning problem.

It must be emphasized, though, that this chapter only deals with some formal solution procedures. Even if, under certain conditions, it can be shown that these procedures will indeed lead to a solution, it remains to be seen what they are worth when it comes to solving practical planning problems. This question will be left unanswered here, since the absence of any experience with this matter would render all attempts speculative.

Although it was argued in chapter 4 that many parameters and constant terms appearing in the traditional planning models will actually be dependent on price changes, we shall restrict ourselves here to the influence of prices on the right-hand-side (RHS) terms. Traditionally these are in multi-sector models the levels of final demands, upper limits for exports, factor supplies, etc. In doing so, we follow the usual practice in general equilibrium theory, but our principal reason is that the problem would be unnecessarily complicated if the general price dependence were taken into consideration. It will be a long time before such an extensive analysis could be applied practically.

The relationship between prices and the RHS terms can be conveniently expressed by price elasticities, so these have to be given in addition to the traditional format that ignores the equilibrium aspect. Suppose now that the traditional model has been set up in the form of a linear programming problem. It will be clear that, after introduction of the price dependence of the RHS terms – even if this can be represented adequately by linear relations – the new, augmented problem will *cease to be linear*. It still remains to be seen in what sense this enlarged programming problem will be different, but, obviously, it will be more elaborate to solve. On the other hand, after the discussion of the general market-equilibrium problem in the previous chapter, the additional complications will prove not to be severe.

Section 6.2. is concerned with the classical approach to solving constrained optimization problems. It introduces briefly the concepts of Lagrangian function and saddle point which will be used in subsequent sections. The nature of the equilibrium programming problem will be examined in section 6.3. The next section discusses the excess-demand algorithm to solve such a problem, and section 6.5. does the same for the excess-price algorithm. The latter section also includes an extensive comparison of both algorithms. When examining the workability of these computation procedures, we shall have a few opportunities to note the close correspondence between the conditions for a stable market equilibrium and those for convergence of the algorithms. Finally, section 6.6. indicates very briefly some other possible solution procedures, among which one approach which is directly related to the planning system of centrally planned economies.

6.2. LAGRANGIAN FUNCTION AND SADDLE POINT

Consider the following constrained optimization problem

$$Dv = \sigma \tag{6.1}$$

$$\text{maximize } f(v'), \tag{6.2}$$

in which vector v $(n \times 1)$ comprises the variables of the system, D $(m \times n)$ is the matrix of coefficients, σ the vector of constant terms, and $f(v)$ stands for the objective function. The classical way to solve this type of problem proceeds by first defining a vector of variables, say π $(m \times 1)$, and then constructing a function, $h(v, \pi)$, such that

$$h(v, \pi) = f(v') + \pi'(Dv - \sigma). \tag{6.3}$$

This is the *Lagrangian function* and the elements of π are called the *Lagrange multipliers*. The function is constructed in such a way that its partial derivatives respect to v and π, if made equal to zero, provide necessary conditions to be satisfied by the point(s) at which $f(v')$ assumes a relative maximum. These conditions are thus

$$\frac{\partial h}{\partial v} = \frac{\partial f}{\partial v} + D'\pi = o \tag{6.4}$$

$$\frac{\partial h}{\partial \pi} = Dv - \sigma = o \tag{6.5}$$

This system contains $m+n$ unknown variables – the v and the π – in $m+n$ equations. The solution procedure is cumbersome, and therefore unattractive from the operational point of view, if the system surpasses the proportions of the simplest type of illustrative example[1]. The reason why the Lagrange multiplier technique is presented here in some detail derives from its value in theoretical proofs.

Observe further that (6.5) is the same as (6.1); it sees to it that the constraints are observed. On the other hand, roughly speaking, (6.4) takes care of optimality. It can also be shown that the Lagrange multipliers are equivalent to our familiar dual prices. Considering the shape of (6.4), this comes rather naturally.

Now let v^0 be a vector among the v satisfying (6.5), at which $f(v^{0\prime})$ takes on a relative maximum and let π^0 be the price vector that corresponds with v^0. It follows that in this case

$$h(v^0, \pi^0) = f(v^{0\prime}) \tag{6.6}$$

since the second term in the Lagrange function drops out. This holds for all vectors which are solutions to (6.5), so in the feasible neighbourhood of (v^0, π^0) we have

$$h(v, \pi^0) = f(v') \le f(v^{0\prime}) = h(v^0, \pi^0) \tag{6.7}$$

with the equality sign holding if $v = v^0$. It also follows from (6.3) that

$$h(v^0, \pi) = f(v^{0\prime}) \tag{6.8}$$

which yields together with (6.7)

$$h(v, \pi^0) \le h(v^0, \pi^0) = h(v^0, \pi). \tag{6.9}$$

This is a special case of a saddle point. In general, a *saddle point* is defined

1. See G. B. DANTZIG, 1963, p. 140 *et seq.* For a more comprehensive treatment of the concepts discussed in this section, see G. HADLEY, 1964.

as the point (v^0, π^0) related to a function $h(v, \pi)$ in the neighbourhood of which the following properties hold

$$h(v, \pi^0) \leq h(v^0, \pi^0) \leq h(v^0, \pi). \tag{6.10}$$

It can easily be shown that a saddle point *implies optimality*. For, if we have the following problem

$$Dv \geq \sigma \tag{6.11}$$

$$\text{maximize } f(v') \tag{6.12}$$

the Lagrange function becomes $h(v, \pi) = f(v') + \pi'(Dv - \sigma)$, where $v \geq 0$ and $\pi \geq 0$. So, (v^0, π^0) is a saddle point of $h(v, \pi)$, if

$$f(v') + \pi^{0'}(Dv - \sigma) \leq f(v^{0'}) + \pi^{0'}(Dv^0 - \sigma) \leq f(v^{0'}) + \pi'(Dv^0 - \sigma). \tag{6.13}$$

With the right-hand inequality, $\pi^0(Dv^0 - \sigma)$ must be equal to zero, since $\pi(Dv^0 - \sigma) \geq 0$. Further, also $\pi^0(Dv - \sigma) \geq 0$. Hence, the first inequality of (6.13) implies that $f(v) \leq f(v^0)$, so v^0 is the optimal vector.

6.3. THE GENERAL-EQUILIBRIUM PROGRAMMING PROBLEM

The general-equilibrium problem is concerned with price-quantity relations, so the Lagrangian function would seem to be particularly useful in this context, for it brings together both items. Specifically, in terms of the symbols employed in the previous section, our problem could be formulated as

$$h(v, \pi) = f(v') + \pi'(Dv - \sigma(\pi)). \tag{6.14}$$

This formulation includes explicitly the relation which exists between the constant terms and the prices which are generated within the system. This is a simplification of course, since it has been emphasized before that there is no reason why price sensitivity should be restricted to the constant terms only. In principle, the objective function and the constraints should allow for the impact of prices as well.

It is clear that (6.14) has a peculiar shape. After introduction of the price dependency, it is no longer an ordinary linear programming problem, even if $f(v')$ were linear. Neither is it a non-linear programming problem, for this class of problems does not include the type of formulation such as we find here, in which the primal form is made dependent on the dual. Hence, problems such as (6.14) form a separate group; let us call them *general-equilibrium programming problems*.

For a moment one may yet suspect that this type of programming problem can simply be solved through its dual form. Our problem is that, if the parameters in the primal form depend on the dual prices, primal variables are mixed with dual variables in the primal form. But this difficulty does not seem to occur in the dual formulation, since the variables of the dual programming problem are, of course, the dual prices. So, if the parameters of this problem were expressed in dual variables, the dual would be a non-linear programming problem. According to this reasoning, the general-equilibrium programming problem would still be only a variant of non-linear programming and not a separate type. This, however, proves to be incorrect which can most easily be explained by way of an example.

Suppose, we are confronted with the following general-equilibrium programming problem

$$x \leq s(p) \qquad ; \qquad s(p) = -\frac{1}{p^3} + 1 \tag{6.15}$$

$$x \geq 0$$

minimize $z = x$

where $p =$ dual variable of corresponding dual formulation. If the above paragraph is correct, the dual problem could be written as

$$p \leq 1 \tag{6.16}$$

$$p \leq 0$$

maximize $v = p\left(-\frac{1}{p^3} + 1\right) = -\frac{1}{p^2} + p$.

For negative values of p – satisfying the constraints of (6.16) – the objective function v peaks at $p = -1.26$, where $v = -1.89$. Substituting this value of p in $s(p)$, we find that $s(p) = 1.5$ which is positive as it should be, in order to allow a solution to (6.15), together with the other constraint. Still, it is evident that z obtains its optimum value at $x = 0$, where $z = 0$. Hence, $z(\text{min}) \neq v(\text{max})$, and (6.16) is apparently *not* the dual of (6.15).

This conclusion leads to a nasty complication, for it would seem to imply that the knowledge available on proofs, characteristics and solution procedures relating to linear and non-linear programming does not help us with the present problem. It may even be necessary to first develop a theory dealing with general equilibrium programming, before any such problem can be tackled.

Fortunately, this predicament will not appear to be as serious as it may seem to be at first sight. Presently two solution procedures will be discussed – in sections 6.4. and 6.5., respectively – by which one version of the general-equilibrium programming problem can be tackled and which rely on concepts which have already become familiar.

6.4. THE CHENERY-KRETSCHMER-UZAWA EXCESS-DEMAND APPROACH

We now come to the presentation of one method with which our equilibrium programming problem can be solved. The origin of the method can be found in an article by CHENERY[2]; it was further elaborated by CHENERY and KRETSCHMER[3] who also sketched a proof of convergence. An extension of the algorithm to other mathematical programming problems and a rigorous proof were provided by CHENERY and UZAWA[4]. Below we shall occupy ourselves only with this last version.

6.4.1. The algorithm

The CHENERY-UZAWA reference model consists partly of a simple multi-sector programming model including among others sectoral balance relations

$$x_i - \sum_j a_{ij} x_j - e_i + m_i = f_i \tag{6.17}$$

with[5] x_i = production of good i $(i = 1, ..., m)$;

a_{ij} = input coefficient from sector i to sector j $(j = 1, ..., m)$;

e_i = exports of product i;

m_i = competitive imports of product i;

f_i = domestic final demand for product i (*dependent on factor and product prices*).

---

2. H. B. CHENERY, 1955.
3. H. B. CHENERY and K. S. KRETSCHMER, 1956.
4. H. B. CHENERY and H. UZAWA, 1958.
5. x_i, e_i and f_i are expressed in quantity units as can be understood from Chenery and Uzawa's presentation. It remains obscure, though, how they can still write that 'the commodity inputs are measured in value terms' and $\sum_i a_{ij} < 1$.

A foreign exchange relation states that the external deficit should not be greater than a pre-fixed amount dictated either by the desire to restrict the disequilibrium on the balance of payments or by the opportunities of obtaining loans from abroad:

$$\Sigma g_j m_j - \Sigma h_j e_j \leq \bar{d} \tag{6.18}$$

where g_j = cost of importing one unit of product j in foreign exchange;
$\quad h_j$ = net revenue in foreign exchange per unit export of good j;
$\quad \bar{d}$ = maximum permissible external deficit in foreign exchange.

Labour supply and demand are given by

$$\Sigma l_j x_j \leq \bar{l} \tag{6.19}$$

where l_j = labour-input coefficient of sector j in man-years;
$\quad \bar{l}$ = manpower population.

Production, exports and imports volumes are required to be non-negative

$$x_j, e_j, m_j \geq 0. \tag{6.20}$$

In this system the revenue *prices of export products* have been made *dependent* on the *volumes* of these products *sold to abroad*, as follows

$$h_j = r_j + s_j e_j \qquad (r_j > 0, s_j < 0). \tag{6.21}$$

Equations (6.21) introduce a price-quantity relation for all export products j so that export-demand functions slope downwards to the right. The objective is to minimize capital requirements

$$\text{minimize } \Sigma k_j x_j \ (\text{maximize} - \Sigma k_j x_j), \tag{6.22}$$

where k_j = capital-input coefficient of sector j.

CHENERY and UZAWA approach the equilibrium problem from a different angle. Their objective is primarily to provide and apply a mathematical programming algorithm, where one of the problems they treat happens to be of the equilibrium programming type. They refer to this aspect only very briefly, whereas this is the very matter which interests us most. Here we shall concentrate on the case in which, in addition to (6.21), the domestic final demand levels f_i are also made dependent on prices.

The *algorithm* consists of the following steps:
1. Adopt non-negative prices for labour and foreign exchange. In the first round CHENERY and UZAWA keep the price of labour low and the exchange rate high in order to make imports unprofitable (see next step),

although this is not strictly necessary. But, otherwise, one may encounter awkward solutions, for example, with positive export and import activities and a zero production activity in one sector, if the price of labour is fixed at a relatively high level.

2. Determine for each sector which activity is to satisfy final demand: domestic production or imports. This is done by comparing the costs of the two activities; for sector j the relevant relations would be

$$p_j = k_j + wl_j + \sum_i a_{ij} p_i \qquad \text{and} \tag{6.23}$$

$$p_j = g_j z \tag{6.24}$$

where $w = $ wage rate;
$\quad z = $ foreign exchange rate.

Eq. (6.23) determines the price of producing commodity j and (6.24) the price of importing it. The lowest-cost activity is selected in the solution. If the two activities are equally profitable, imports are preferred.

The reader may have noticed that this procedure requires a triangular input-output table which is arranged in such a way that all sectors only put in their own products and goods from sectors which appear lower in the table. It appears that rather many input-output tables can be arranged to possess this property or to come very close to it[6]. In such a table the criterion indicated by (6.23) and (6.24) can be applied without difficulty: starting with the last sector and working backwards, the prices of input products from other sectors (p_i) – whether imported or produced domestically – are known, since they have been determined in previous calculations. In a non-triangular input-output table this simple approach would not work, which complicates the calculations. CHENERY and UZAWA provide a recursive formula to cope with this situation.

3. The domestic cost prices of commodities j allow assessment of the level of exports, since for (6.21) may be written

$$p_j^r = z r_j + z s_j e_j \tag{6.25}$$

if $p_j^r = $ revenue price of export good j in domestic currency. It follows that the marginal revenue of export product j can be given by

$$\frac{d(e_j p_j^r)}{de_j} = z r_j + 2 z s_j e_j. \tag{6.26}$$

6. See, for example, H. B. CHENERY and T. WATANABE, 1958, and D. SIMPSON and J. TSUKUI, 1965.

In order to maximize profits on exporting good j this expression should be made equal to the marginal costs of producing it (p_j). The relevant export level thus becomes

$$e_j = \frac{p_j - zr_j}{2zs_j}. \tag{6.27}$$

Negative values of exports are incompatible with (6.20) and are replaced by a zero activity level.

4. In the present case, where the domestic final demand levels are also dependent on prices, a similar calculation as in step 3 must be carried out so as to find the final demands. For this purpose we must know the relation between the two sets of items. In general:

$$f_i = f_i(p_1, ..., p_m, w, z). \tag{6.28}$$

5. From the previous steps total final demand levels can now be established. It is also known for each sector whether its product is to be supplied domestically or from abroad, so the volumes of production or imports can be determined without difficulty.

6. The sum of all import outlays can presently be compared with total export revenues determined in the third step to find the external deficit that would result under the prices assumed to hold for labour and foreign exchange in step 1. Similarly, demand for labour can be assessed with the help of (6.19).

7. If demand for foreign exchange as calculated in the previous step surpasses supply allowed by (6.18) (excess demand), the exchange rate is raised. In the case of excess supply, the exchange rate is lowered. The same procedure is applied *mutatis mutandis* to labour and the wage rate according to (6.19). The next iteration repeats this process of calculations on the basis of the new prices for the two primary products, and so on, until the need for price adaptations has been eliminated when either demand for and supply of labour and foreign exchange have become equal, or excess supply still prevails although the prices of both factors have dropped to zero, or a combination of these cases has been reached.

The final solution is obviously the equilibrium solution that we are looking for. Further, at each stage, and therefore also in the final solution, capital outlays are minimized, for, with the in-prices of labour and foreign exchange given, the selection of the supply activity in step 2 is ultimately determined by the capital costs.

When studying this algorithm, one cannot fail to notice how closely it resembles the excess-demand adaptation pattern towards general equilibrium presented in subsection 5.4.3. This is, of course, not a coincidence. This wellknown adaptation pattern must have inspired the application of the same basic principles to the present problem. One may expect that other adaptation patterns will lend themselves for translation into such algorithms too.

6.4.2. Convergence of the excess-demand approach

Hence, the algorithm operates along the following lines: departing from arbitrary initial prices for labour and foreign exchange, the commodity prices are determined uniquely. This set of prices is used for two purposes, namely to calculate the final demand vector, and to decide the way in which this demand is to be satisfied, by selecting for each good the activity which 'prices the other out', very much like the simplex method using multipliers (G. B. DANTZIG, *ibid.*, p. 216). By the fact that in-prices – and therefore also the final demand volumes – are prefixed in each round of calculations, the problem is *linear* in each iteration. The objective of the iteration process is to find a *feasible* solution, that is, an optimum/ equilibrium solution.

It remains to be shown that the algorithm indeed leads to such a solution. Doing so, we shall encounter once more a few analogies with the proof concerning stability of the general equilibrium. In the proof[7] use is made of the theorem by which the global optimum of a mathematical programming problem must coincide with the global saddle point solution of its corresponding Lagrangian function, such that in order to find the former, it suffices to locate the latter (section 6.2.).

So let us now form the Lagrangian of the reference model (6.17) to (6.22):

$$h(v, \pi) = -\Sigma k_j x_j + \sum_j p_j(-f_j(p_j, z, w) + x_j - \sum_i a_{ji} x_i - e_j + m_j) +$$
$$+ z(\bar{d} - \Sigma g_j m_j + \Sigma h_j e_j) + w(\bar{l} - \Sigma l_j x_j). \tag{6.29}$$

Price dependence in (6.29) is restricted to two groups, namely the e_j and the $f_j(p_j, z, w)$. If there is one vector $v(\pi)$ that maximizes $h(v, \pi)$ for a given vector π, it follows that $h(v^0, \pi) \le h(v(\pi), \pi)$, and if $h(v, \pi)$ has a

---

7. H. B. CHENERY and H. UZAWA, *ibid.*

saddle point at (v^0, π^0) we also have that $h(v, \pi^0) \le h(v^0, \pi^0)$. Writing out these relations in full, adding up and taking into account (6.17), (6.18), (6.19) and non-negativity of z and w, these conditions imply that

$$(z^0 - z)(\bar{d} - \Sigma g_j m_j + \Sigma h_j e_j) + (w^0 - w)(\bar{l} - \Sigma l_j x_j) \le$$
$$\le \Sigma (p_j^0 - p_j)(f_j^0 - f_j), \tag{6.30}$$

where $f_j^0 = f_j(p_j^0, z^0, w^0)$, $f_j = f_j(p_j, z, w)$ and where upper index o indicates the optimum, as before.

Again we note the *correspondence* with one stage of the *equilibrium analysis* that led to the formulation of relation (5.25). In the terms of the model that we are now dealing with, it would have read

$$\Sigma (p_j^0 - p_j)(f_j^0 - f_j) - (z^0 - z)(d^0 - d) - (w^0 - w)(l^0 - l) \le 0 \tag{5.25'}$$

with $d^0 =$ supply of foreign exchange under price vector (p_j^0, z^0, w^0);
$d \ =$ supply of foreign exchange under price vector (p_j, z, w) and similarly for l.

The differences result from the fact that the equilibrium problem compares two different factor supplies that depend on prices, whereas the programming problem compares a fixed supply with variable demand levels. This difference also causes the opposing signs. Recall, however, that relation (5.25) has been derived, assuming that the conditions for stability of the general equilibrium are satisfied, whereas (6.30) appears to hold, if $h(v, \pi)$ possesses a saddle point.

In the proof of convergence towards general equilibrium (5.4.3.), we made use of the direct relation between factor prices and product prices. By this property, the adaptation pattern – which ran in terms of factor prices – could also be expressed in product prices, so that (5.25) became applicable. In the present problem, however, there is scope for choice between import prices and domestic prices (step 2).

Therefore, another condition is introduced, namely

$$\Sigma (p_j^0 - p_j)(f_j^0 - f_j) \le 0. \tag{6.31}$$

From earlier experience we know that this implies 'dominating' substitution effects in the final demand functions. Substituting (6.31) in (6.30), we get

$$(z^0 - z)(\bar{d} - \Sigma g_j m_j + \Sigma h_j e_j) + (w^0 - w)(\bar{l} - \Sigma l_j x_j) \le 0. \tag{6.32}$$

The remaining part of this proof is very similar to the proof in 5.4.3., so it can be sketched very briefly.

In symbols, the present method of successive adaptation can be represented as follows

$$k\dot{z} = \begin{cases} 0, \text{ if } z = 0 \text{ and } \Sigma g_j m_j - \Sigma h_j e_j < \bar{d} \\ \Sigma g_j m_j - \Sigma h_j e_j - \bar{d}, \text{ otherwise} \end{cases} \tag{6.33}$$

$$k\dot{w} = \begin{cases} 0, \text{ if } w = 0 \text{ and } \Sigma l_j x_j < \bar{l} \\ \Sigma l_j x_j - \bar{l}, \text{ otherwise} \end{cases} \tag{6.34}$$

where k – a positive number – also takes care of the different units on either side of the equality signs. Now define a new variable v such that

$$2v = (z^0 - z)^2 k + (w^0 - w)^2 k. \text{ Therefore} \tag{6.35}$$

$$\dot{v} = (z^0 - z) k\dot{z} - (w^0 - w) k\dot{w}. \tag{6.36}$$

From this equation together with (6.32), (6.33), (6.36) and positivity of k, it follows that $\dot{v} \leq 0$, where $\dot{v} = 0$, if $z = z^0$ and $w = w^0$. Hence, as long as $z \neq z^0$ and $w \neq w^0$, $v > 0$, although under these conditions $\dot{v} < 0$. But then v approaches its limit of zero and factor prices converge to their optimum/ equilibrium values. When that point has been reached, the adaptation process comes to an end, since the attainment of the optimum implies that either $z = 0$ with $\Sigma g_j m_j - \Sigma h_j e_j < \bar{d}$, or $\Sigma g_j m_j - \Sigma h_j e_j = \bar{d}$, so that $\dot{z} = 0$, and where a similar reasoning holds for the wage adaptations.

6.4.3. The limits of the adaptation coefficient

Let us now examine more closely the value of the *adaptation coefficient* in the context of the above solution method[8]. Since our investigation will allow, in the first instance, for different adaptation coefficients for different factor prices, the iterative method has been slightly reformulated. If we generalize the algorithm in this way and express it in difference equations, (6.33) and (6.34) can be written as

$$v_{t+1} = \max \{o, v_t + K(\delta(v_t) - \rho)\} \tag{6.37}$$

where v_{t+1} = vector of prices of production factors imposed in the $t + 1$st round;

K = matrix with adaptation coefficients > 0 on the main diagonal; other elements zero;

$\delta(v_t)$ = vector of demand levels for factors in round t; indirectly dependent on factor prices (see algorithm);

ρ = levels of factor supplies (constant).

8. See H. UZAWA, 1958.

From (6.37) it follows that we can write

$$|v_{t+1}|^2 \leq |v_t|^2 + |K(\delta(v_t) - \rho)|^2 + 2\{K(\delta(v_t) - \rho)\}' v_t. \tag{6.38}$$

This formulation introduces the concept of distances between vectors. For example, the distance between vector α and vector β is defined as $|\alpha - \beta| = \{(\alpha - \beta)'(\alpha - \beta)\}^{\frac{1}{2}}$. Consequently, $|v_{t+1}|^2$ in (6.38) indicates the square of the distance between v_{t+1} and the zero vector, etc.

In a similar notation

$$|v_t - v^0|^2 = |v_t|^2 + |v^0|^2 - 2v_t' v^0 \qquad \text{and} \tag{6.39}$$

$$|v_{t+1} - v^0|^2 = |v_{t+1}|^2 + |v^0|^2 - 2v_{t+1}' v^0. \tag{6.40}$$

Substituting (6.38) in (6.40), we get

$$|v_{t+1} - v^0|^2 \leq |v_t|^2 + |K(\delta(v_t) - \rho)|^2 + 2\{K(\delta(v_t) - \rho)\}' v_t + |v^0|^2 -$$
$$- 2v_{t+1}' v^0. \tag{6.41}$$

From (6.37) it can further be derived that

$$-2v_{t+1}' v^0 \leq -2v_t' v^0 - 2\{K(\delta(v_t) - \rho)\}' v^0 \tag{6.42}$$

and if this expression is substituted in (6.41) while making use of (6.39), we have

$$|v_{t+1} - v^0|^2 \leq |v_t - v^0|^2 + |K(\delta(v_t) - \rho)|^2 + 2\{K(\delta(v_t) - \rho)\}'(v_t - v^0). \tag{6.43}$$

Hence, monotonous convergence of the vector of factor prices towards their optimum/equilibrium values is warranted, if

$$|K(\delta(v_t) - \rho)|^2 + 2\{K(\delta(v_t) - \rho)\}'(v_t - v^0) \leq 0. \tag{6.44}$$

This is as far as we can go, as long as we insist on different adaptation coefficients for different factors of production. The value or value range of each of these coefficients cannot be derived from this relation. A few more steps can be made, however, if this requirement is dropped. With one common adaptation coefficient namely, say k, the equivalent of (6.44) would have become

$$k^2 |\delta(v_t) - \rho|^2 + 2k(\delta(v_t) - \rho)'(v_t - v^0) \leq 0 \tag{6.44'}$$

Neglecting the futile solution of $k = 0$, we find that k must fulfil the following condition

$$k \leq -\frac{2(\delta(v_t) - \rho)'(v_t - v^0)}{|\delta(v_t) - \rho|^2} \qquad (k > 0) \tag{6.45}$$

The RHS form is positive, since, by (6.32), its numerator is negative if $v_t \neq v^0$. So k has indeed a positive range, as the reasoning under (6.36) requires.

We have now found that the present iterative method will eventually lead towards a stable optimum/equilibrium solution if certain conditions are fulfilled and the correction coefficient does not surpass a certain limit. Unfortunately, this value can only be found if the solution values are known in advance, which confirms our earlier suspicions. The progress that we have made consists of the formal demonstration that the range of values which k may assume is indeed *limited*. It also follows from (6.45) that this range varies through the iterations. However, it does not help us to specify the upper limit of that range which would have been a useful piece of information in the solution procedure. One of the conclusions of the previous chapter, namely that the problem of selecting the adjustment coefficient must be tackled gingerly, remains fully intact.

6.5. THE EXCESS-PRICE APPROACH

We have seen that the version of the equilibrium programming problem, as formulated in the previous section, can indeed be solved if certain conditions regarding the price-quantity relations are satisfied. Until now we have only been concerned with the solution of the equilibrium aspect of this problem. But it will be clear that the other aspect, viz. the existence of restrictions to price variations, can easily be built into the procedure, by taking into account certain price constraints in those steps of the algorithm where the dual prices are determined. Therefore, with the present tools, it should be possible to carry out now the exercise presented in the next chapter. But it will be worth examining an alternative approach first. This will be done in this section.

The alternative procedure proposed here is based on the excess-price approach that has been outlined at an earlier stage and which has been applied in the numerical example of chapter 5. In a few words, it consists of the successive adaptation of imposed prices, determining the parameters (the in-prices) in the direction of the dual prices in the solution of the relevant programming problem (the out-prices) in the previous round. The rationale of this approach has already been mentioned, so it will not be necessary to repeat it here. Formally, its pattern of adaptation can be described as follows

$$\hat{\pi}_t = \hat{\pi}_{t-1} + k(\pi_{t-1} - \hat{\pi}_{t-1}), \qquad \hat{\pi}_t \geq 0; \qquad 0 < k < 1 \tag{6.46}$$

in which $\hat{\pi}_t =$ the vector of prices imposed in round t (in-prices);
$\pi_t =$ the vector of prices calculated in round t (out-prices);
$k =$ the adaptation coefficient.

It may be clarifying to interpret the in-prices as the prices that are *expected* to hold during a certain period on the basis of which certain decisions are taken (determining the RHS vector). In order to comply with these decisions, the economy (the model) adjusts the levels of its economic activities, and the actual prices (out-prices) going with this economic structure may well differ from the expected prices. In as far as this is the case, the initial price outlook is belied by the 'facts' and this experience influences the level of prices expected for the next period, resulting in upward or downward adjustments, as the case may be. In this way, price expectations become the reflection of a series of weighted price observations relating to previous periods. The next formula shows this very clearly, since (6.46) can be rewritten as

$$\hat{\pi}_t = k \sum_{r=1}^{t-1} (1-k)^{t-1-r}\pi_r + (1-k)^{t-1}\hat{\pi}_1 . \tag{6.47}$$

Since $0 < k < 1$, it follows that recent experience counts more in the formation of expectations than past experience, which is very reasonable.

If we view the problem in this way, the excess-price algorithm happens to coincide practically with CAGAN's adaptive expectations hypothesis in a variant of KOYCK's distributed lags analysis[9]. Although this hypothesis is concerned with the effects of hyperinflation, its principle of revising the expected value of a variable proportionally to the difference between the actual value and the value expected previously, is exactly the same.

In chapter 5, when discussing dynamic adaptation patterns, we had an opportunity for a brief, tentative comparison of the excess-demand and excess-price approaches. In the present section this comparison will be extended in the context of a programming problem. We are particularly interested in a. how far excess prices imply excess demands and *vice versa* (subsection 6.5.1.) and, b. which are the properties that the two approaches have in common and, c. how far each of the remaining properties may possibly render one method more favourable than the other (subsection 6.5.3.). Convergence of the excess-price algorithm will be examined in 6.5.2. For simplicity's sake it will be assumed that only the RHS vector varies with prices.

9. P. D. CAGAN, 1956, and L. M. KOYCK, 1954. See also K. F. WALLIS, 1969, for a comparative study of their dynamic models and those of other authors. For other price-expectation patterns in the context of equilibrium analysis, see R. E. KUENNE, 1963, chapter 8.

6.5.1. Dual prices and excess demand

A large part of the relations in traditional, multi-sector planning models often consists of *confrontations of demand and supply volumes*, where one of the two volumes is given, either as a fixed amount or as a range of permissible values and where the other has to adapt itself accordingly. In some relations demand is predetermined, e.g. domestic final demand, and demand for export products. The solution has to make sure that supply is large enough to cope with it. In other relations the supply side of the market is given, e.g. supply of capital and foreign exchange, so in this case the solution values of demand for these items are to adapt themselves to these magnitudes. Some simple multi-sector models are entirely composed of such relations, such as the reference model of the foregoing section. (Evidently, this is not a coincidence, since the solution method presented there is precisely based on the possibility of direct confrontation of demand and supply.)

It is important to realize what this implies for the prices corresponding to these relations. It follows that imposed prices – which determine the values of the parameters – and dual prices not only have different functions in a programming model, they also refer to different sides of the market. In order to clarify this point let us take, for example, final demand for a certain commodity. When deciding on the magnitude of this item – appearing as an RHS constant in most planning models which treat it separately – we must make some assumptions regarding its main determinants, amongst other things, the price of the commodity. The latter is, therefore, a *demand price*. On the other hand, the corresponding dual price of that commodity is a cost price, or a *supply price*, namely the price at which this very amount of final demand can be satisfied, by domestic production or by imports.

Instances of the other case, where the supply side is given, are rarer in multi-sector models. Available volumes of factors of production are often treated as such, but we have observed already that, for different reasons, supply of capital, labour and foreign exchange is hardly affected by the rate of interest, the wage rate and the rate of exchange. However, this may be different for the land factor. The rent level, will, for instance, determine the area of land offered for economic use, which could appear as an RHS constant in a multi-sector model. This time the in-price (the rent) would be a *supply price*. But the corresponding dual price indicates the price that land users are willing to pay for it. Hence, this would be a *demand price*.

Therefore, if the excess-demand approach compares levels of demand

and supply at a certain price level, the excess-price approach compares demand prices with supply prices at a certain quantity level[10]. Consequently, the latter differs from the former in the sense that it views the problem and approaches the solution from a different angle, a characterization that becomes literally true if the two methods are represented graphically, as in graph 5.2. for the simple market-equilibrium case. Or, expressed alternatively, for the gradual approximation of the equilibrium, one method relies on quantity information and the other on price information, whereas both variables *together* determine the equilibrium position.

Since the excess-price method steers on information regarding the observed difference between imposed and dual prices, it will be interesting to examine the effects on the magnitudes in the primal solution if valuation of constraints in a programming problem were based on imposed, rather than on dual prices. In order to be able to do so, let us first consider what dual prices stand for.

First recall how dual prices are defined. Multiplying dual prices by the input coefficients of corresponding rows and adding by columns (activities) give figures which – for the basic activities – are precisely equal to the coefficients in the objective function. For the non-basic activities the sums are larger than, or, at best, equal to the cost coefficients in a maximizing problem, or smaller than, or, at best, equal to them in a minimizing problem. This derives from the fact that the optimal values attached to inputs (costs) and outputs (revenues) as indicated by the dual prices allow only the 'best' activities to just break even. None of the other activities can do better than that, so they are not allowed to operate, as this would necessarily lead away from the optimum solution – in an upward or downward direction, as the case may be.

However, a valuation system which differs only slightly from the dual set will *completely disrupt* the above-described regularities: the basic activities may become profitable, or may start to operate at a loss, but they will probably no longer assume exactly the neutral position. Non-basic activities, on the other hand, may become more or less unprofitable, or may altogether cease to be unattractive. As a consequence, the activities appearing in the basis under two different scales of valuation in the same problem may have little in common. Not only will the variables themselves be different, but the numbers of activities that are worth executing

10. Recall also the numerical example of the previous chapter and the subsequent derivation of its equilibrium conditions for an illustration of the feature that imposed prices and dual prices represent different sides of the market.

according to each price set may differ too. Further, except for price sets that correspond with feasible solutions, one or more constraints will be violated.

These conclusions are all self-evident, since they spring directly from the nature of dual prices, but they also help to supply better understanding of how the excess-demand and the excess-price approach are related. The latter starts by assuming a set of prices (demand and supply prices, as indicated by the nature of the RHS constants they refer to) and fixes these constants accordingly, then proceeds to determine the optimal solution, in which all demand levels and corresponding supply components have become equal and that also gives the dual counterparts (supply and demand prices, respectively) of the imposed prices.

According to the characterization given above, the *excess-demand approach* would also first decide on the prices to be used for the assessment of the RHS vector, but from then on it would sail a different course. The leading principle of this method is that it insists on one and the same price at *both sides* of the market. Hence, it does *not* permit the dual prices to seek their optimal value, since they may deviate, sometimes even widely, from the in-prices. So evaluation of the constraints has to be based on these imposed prices instead. What such a deviation from the dual set implies for the optimal solution has just been indicated. Clearly, there is no reason now to expect that the supply and demand values in the RHS vector will be exactly met by demand and supply activities in the 'solution'[11] to the problem. Without prior information, a solution with matching levels of supply and demand would be a case of sheer luck, well deserved sometimes, but highly unlikely to occur. Normally there will be excess demand for and excess supply of a number of items.

Let us now examine whether the two approaches will steer the adjustments to be made in the next stage in the same direction, if they start from the same initial position (same problem, same imposed prices). In principle, there are *four different cases* to be considered, since (i) the out-prices will be either larger or smaller than the in-prices and (ii) they will be either offer or demand prices. Since the arguments in each case will be basically similar, it will suffice, however, to deal with only one case in some detail.

So let us examine, for example, whether there are reasons to expect an excess demand for an item, if, in the excess-price approach, its demand in-price falls short of its supply out-price. Since the dual price is the one

---

11. A true solution is not really possible and some adaptations are required. We come back to this below.

which ensures that supply equates demand under zero profits, it seems rather obvious that a price lower than that in the excess-demand approach will force the activity which supplies the item into the red, so that it will have to drop out. Furthermore, the lower-than-dual price will make the item a more attractive input which will stimulate demand for it. Hence, if there is a tendency, it will be in the direction of an excess demand. Since this result will lead to an increase in the imposed price of this item in the next round, *the two approaches would run parallel*, because also the excess-price method would raise that price on the basis of the higher dual price.

This may seem rather convincing, but, unfortunately, there are some difficulties. For example, the other prices in the imposed set may result in such low cost items that this may still save the activity. Even if this is not the case, they may render another activity attractive which is also capable of supplying the relevant item, so it can replace the original one. These two possibilities may seem unlikely to occur in an actual problem; still the relation between excess-price and excess-demand approach becomes somewhat uncertain. The same holds for a comparison of the other possible outcomes of both approaches: there is a definite tendency towards concurrence, but some factors may disturb this pattern (evidently, they may also strengthen it).

This comparison ended rather inconclusively because this particular version of the excess-demand approach was unable to decide between excess demand or supply, let alone arrive at a firm indication of the size of the excess. This resulted again from the *incoherence* of the *imposed prices*, so that the set of activities which were sufficiently attractive to become operational under this scheme of valuation also lacked coherence. There is, for example, no good reason to anticipate that all necessary inputs in the model will indeed be provided: the relevant activities may not be profitable. Therefore, it may be even premature to examine whether the execution of an activity will be worth while on the basis of the imposed prices, when it has not yet been established that the necessary inputs will indeed be available.

The ambiguity that characterizes this version of the excess-demand approach has been overcome by the CHENERY-UZAWA algorithm. As we have seen, this method succeeds in finding a determinate solution by imposing in each iteration *only* the *prices of the factors* of production. Then the product prices are derived from them to obtain a coherent price set. The method thus becomes a curtailed excess-demand approach, since the excess demands and supplies are limited to production factors only. This version cannot be compared, however, with the excess-price method,

104

since the requirement regarding the interconnection of the in-prices does not occur in the latter approach. And because the points of departure differ from each other, the adjustments cannot be compared either.

One can imagine still *another version of the excess-demand procedure,* namely one that examines the effect of equating the demand and supply prices one by one, while other prices are left free to settle at the level where demand (supply) meets prefixed supply (demand). In terms of a programming model one would first find the solution and then set the dual prices one by one equal to the imposed prices. Thereafter it can be determined whether this operation would result in an excess demand or supply of the relevant item. Suppose now that the imposed price replacing the dual price of one item exceeds the latter. A natural tendency will then arise towards an increase in supply of that item and/or a decrease in demand for it, that is, a tendency towards excess supply. As a consequence, the price imposed in the next round would be fixed lower. Obviously, the excess-price approach would do just the same on the basis of the direct observation that the dual price falls short of the imposed price. Similarly, replacing a dual price by a lower imposed price will cause a tendency towards excess demand so that the next pre-assigned price of that item will be fixed at a higher level. Thus, this particular version of the excess-demand approach proves to coincide exactly with the excess-price method.

6.5.2. *Towards a proof of convergence of the excess-price approach*

Although the excess-price algorithm corresponds with the excess-demand approach, we must still examine the former's conditions for convergence. So let us consider the following system which expresses the general equilibrium problem according to the excess-price approach:

$$Dv = \sigma(\hat{\pi}) \qquad\qquad (i = 1, ..., m; \; m < n) \qquad\qquad (6.48)$$

$$\text{maximize } f(v'), \qquad\qquad\qquad (6.49)$$

where D $(m \times n)$ is the matrix of coefficients, where the meaning of the other symbols and the dimension of the vectors are the same as in 6.2., and where $\hat{\pi}$ (≥ 0) stands for the vector of in-prices. The items to which prices in π and $\hat{\pi}$ relate are the same. In each iteration, the problem is a simple linear programming problem and the corresponding Lagrangian function is

$$h(v, \pi) = f(v') + \pi'(Dv - \sigma(\hat{\pi})). \qquad\qquad (6.50)$$

The task now is to find the saddle point of $h(v, \pi, \hat{\pi})$ in v and π, for a given $\hat{\pi}$, where also exists *equality between π and $\hat{\pi}$*. This particular saddle point – in symbols (v^0, π^0) – indicates an optimum as well as an equilibrium.

Let σ be a vector of final demand items, expressed in physical terms, which depend on prices in vector $\hat{\pi}$, and suppose that the relations between the two are such that 'substitution effects dominate'. We know from subsection 5.4.3. that in that case we have

$$(\pi_1 - \pi_2)'(\sigma_1 - \sigma_2) < 0, \tag{6.51}$$

where $\pi_1 \neq \pi_2$ and $\sigma_1 = \sigma(\pi_1)$ and $\sigma_2 = \sigma(\pi_2)$. In addition to this we have information regarding the adaptation pattern which is characteristic for the algorithm. It reads

$$\frac{d\hat{\pi}}{dt} = k(\pi - \hat{\pi}), \qquad 0 < k < 1. \tag{6.52}$$

Taking the derivative of $(\hat{\pi} - \pi^0)'(\hat{\sigma} - \sigma^0)$ with respect to time, we get

$$\frac{d}{dt}((\hat{\pi} - \pi^0)'(\hat{\sigma} - \sigma^0)) = (\hat{\sigma} - \sigma^0)'\frac{d\hat{\pi}}{dt} + (\hat{\pi} - \pi^0)'\frac{d\hat{\sigma}}{d\hat{\pi}}\frac{d\hat{\pi}}{dt} = \tag{6.53}$$

$$= k(\hat{\sigma} - \sigma^0)'(\pi - \hat{\pi}) + k(\hat{\pi} - \pi^0)'\frac{d\hat{\sigma}}{d\hat{\pi}}(\pi - \hat{\pi}). \tag{6.53'}$$

Given our assumption regarding the market behaviour of the final demand items, we have $(\hat{\pi} - \pi^0)'(\hat{\sigma} - \sigma^0) < 0$, if $\hat{\pi} \neq \pi^0$. Hence, it follows from experience with similar problems in 5.4.3. and 6.4.2. that it suffices to show that (6.53') is positive for a proof of convergence of the present algorithm.

For a certain vector of in-prices $\hat{\pi}$ $(\hat{\pi} \neq \pi^0)$, v optimizes $h(v, \pi, \hat{\pi})$, so

$$f(v') \geq f(v^{0'}) + \pi'(Dv^0 - \sigma(\hat{\pi})). \tag{6.54}$$

On the other hand, v^0 maximizes $h(v, \pi^0, \pi^0)$, and therefore

$$f(v^{0'}) \geq f(v') + \pi^{0'}(Dv - \sigma(\pi^0)). \tag{6.55}$$

Adding up (6.54) and (6.55), and taking into account (6.48), we obtain

$$(\pi - \pi^0)'(\hat{\sigma} - \sigma^0) \geq 0. \tag{6.56}$$

Further, $(\hat{\pi} - \pi^0)'(\hat{\sigma} - \sigma^0) < 0$ as long as $\hat{\pi} \neq \pi^0$. This, together with (6.56), gives

$$(\pi - \hat{\pi})'(\hat{\sigma} - \sigma^0) > 0. \tag{6.57}$$

So the first term of (6.53') is indeed positive outside the equilibrium position.

The second term poses greater problems. Rewriting it, we get

$$k(\hat{\pi}-\pi^0)'\frac{d\hat{\sigma}}{d\hat{\pi}}(\pi-\hat{\pi}) = k(\hat{\pi}-\pi^0)'\frac{d\hat{\sigma}}{d\hat{\pi}}(\pi^0-\quad)+k(\hat{\pi}-\pi^0)'\frac{d\hat{\sigma}}{d\hat{\pi}}(\pi-\pi^0).$$
(6.58)

What makes this equality interesting is that it contains the expression $d\hat{\sigma}/d\hat{\pi}$ which describes the derivatives of the final demand items with respect to the vector of in-prices. It is not hard to see that they form a Jacobian matrix of the type discussed rather extensively in 5.4.3. This matrix played an important role there in the proof of convergence towards the *general equilibrium point*. Specifically it was demonstrated that under 'dominating substitution effects', the quadratic form $\lambda'J\lambda$ was negative, and this proved to be instrumental for the dynamic, excess-demand adaptation pattern to converge. Here we encounter the negative of this form again in the guise of the first term right of the quality sign in (6.58).

This is an important conclusion, since it builds a *bridge* between two essential elements of the analysis. It is also a helpful finding, for, given the supposed behaviour of final demand, it implies that the first term on the right hand side of (6.58) is *positive* as long as $\hat{\pi} \neq \pi^0$.

The second term, however, is undetermined in sign. Clearly, if $\hat{\pi}-\pi^0 = = \pi^0-\pi$, this term would be positive as well. This would occur, if the equilibrium-price vector lay exactly between the vectors of in-prices and out-prices. Although in section 4.4. it was tentatively argued that there might be a tendency for equilibrium prices to end up indeed somewhere between these two vectors, this is, of course, not sufficient for positivity of the second term right of (6.58).

Summing up the argument, it can be concluded that of the three terms into which (6.53) has been broken down, two can be shown to be positive, whereas the remaining term is undeterminate. If the weight and sign of the latter are not such that it outweighs the other two – and this seems hardly likely – the sign of (6.53) is indeed as it should be for convergence of the excess-price algorithm towards the optimum/equilibrium point.

6.5.3. A comparison of the two algorithms

It turned out to be impossible to relate to each other the excess demands in CHENERY's factor-excess-demand algorithm and the excess prices in the alternative method. But some of the other characteristics can indeed be compared, as will presently be done.

The obstacle which stood in the way of a direct comparison derived from the coherence of factor and product in-prices required in the excess-demand method. So, in order to concentrate on the differences between the processes in the two approaches that generate the information leading to adjustments in the next round, let us assume that both start with the same coherent, but not yet equilibrated initial price set[12] and, therefore, also the same RHS vector. Hence, the two initial formats are identical *and* satisfy the coherence requirement. Setting out to find the excess demands and supplies that this price set gives rise to, one would first determine the activities that are to satisfy final demand for the various commodities. These variables are selected on the basis of the initial prices, so there is an inevitable bias in favour of activities that use relatively much (little) – directly plus indirectly – of the factors that are undervalued (overvalued) relative to their equilibrium prices and/or which produce relatively little (much) of the factors that are priced too low (high). Obviously, the same criterion selects against activities with an opposite structure. As a consequence, the underpriced factors will tend to be in excess demand, whereas overvalued factors will end up with supply surpassing demand, so the adaptations will point in the right direction.

In the excess-price method, however, demand and supply of all relevant items should meet exactly, implying that it will have to seek a set of activities *different* from the one that the excess-demand procedure produced. The latter, though satisfying the final demand levels, violated the primary factor constraints, since the initial prices differed from the equilibrium set. Hence, in order to match demand and supply of primary factors as well, the present basis will lean towards activities that either economize on factors that are in excess demand in the other solution and/or make considerable use of factors with an excess of supply. The dual prices in the counterpart of this primal solution will necessarily reflect this tendency; the dual price of the factor with too high a demand in the excess-demand approach will tend to be on the high side in the excess-price approach in order to compete a number of activities 'out of the market' and, thereby, to curtail demand, or to stimulate supply. On the other hand, factors in over-supply in one approach will tend to have low dual prices in the other.

There is nothing in this reasoning that guarantees a perfect parallelism of the successive adjustments of the two methods under the same coherent

12. Thus, the term 'coherent' is used in this context to indicate that product in-prices are in accordance with factor in-prices (step 2 of the excess-demand algorithm). 'Equilibrated' refers, of course, to the situation where in-prices equal out-prices.

price set, but the tendency will probably be very strong. It is interesting to observe, though, that this is achieved with opposite appreciation for the cost structures of the activities.

It can further be seen that the excess-demand approach is almost entirely consistent throughout the iterations, with the exception of the prices of prime factors. For these items demand and supply do not yet match before the point of convergence, but for the others they do, and at levels concurrent with the ruling price set. But the problem is continuously *infeasible* except for the final round. The alternative algorithm, on the other hand, has a feasible solution in each round, but now *price inconsistency* indicates that the final solution has not yet been reached. This is another difference between the two methods. They agree again in their attempts to acquire the property that the other method possesses – or nearly possesses – already. It follows that the final solution for both is the one that is feasible *and* consistent at the same time.

The properties that we have so far discussed, although they distinguish the two methods from each other, do not yet allow a comparison of their various advantages and disadvantages. Indeed, on the basis of the criterion whether one method is rendered more easily understandable and/or applicable than the other, they appear to be neutral. But from the point of view of efficiency of the calculation procedure, the excess-price method may have some advantages over the excess-demand approach.

First, a point in favour of the excess-price algorithm is that its adjustment mechanism is exclusively concerned with prices, whereas the other one has to translate a difference between two quantities into a price adaptation. In the latter case it will be more difficult to decide on the measure in which the pre-assigned prices have to be altered. The extents of the price excesses, however, by their very nature provide a direct indication.

Second, a presumably more important advantage of the method proposed here is its relative simplicity in practical application, since, from iteration to iteration, the problem to be solved is only of the ordinary linear programming type[13]. The number of calculations to be performed per iteration in each of the two methods is only of relatively small interest here as there is no significant difference in this respect. But the fact that solving linear programming problems has become a routine operation, seems to lend the excess-price method some advantage over the other

13. Admittedly, this advantage only applies if indeed the problem ignoring price consistency is linear. If this is not the case, the excess-price approach loses much of its attraction for a practical exercise.

method which employs a less conventional approach. In particular computer facilities can, therefore, be utilized better when the excess-price algorithm is applied.

6.6. CONCLUDING REMARKS

In the previous sections attention has been called to the close similarities in principle and in appearance between the programming problems and their solution procedures discussed there on the one hand, and other subjects in different fields of economics or mathematical economics on the other, namely the general market equilibrium and the price behaviour under hyperinflation. Let us now consider the resemblance between the above algorithms for equilibrium programming problems and those applied to a relatively new branch of mathematical programming, namely that concerned with decomposable programmes.

The decomposition principle in mathematical programming[14] derives from the fact that in programming problems certain parts are sometimes largely independent of each other. The independent portions are called the subprogrammes and the part indicating the interconnections is the masterprogramme. This type of problem may arise when the activity levels of different units are to be co-ordinated.

Two-level-planning[15], for example, is concerned with such problems. In this set-up, a central authority co-ordinates the activities of the productive units. It ensures that the available means are allocated in such a way that the overall requirements are met, while a common objective is optimized. The problem is solved in a number of stages. In each stage tentative prices are assigned to factors and products, and the production units accordingly determine their optimal levels of activity and how much they will buy and sell of each item. This information is passed back to the centre which can then compare the overall effects of its instructions with the corresponding constraints. On the basis of the observed discrepancies, it can issue new price directives, and so on, until all inconsistencies have been eliminated.

This brief description reveals that the input-output structure in this system is expressly consistent with the ruling price set (see J. KORNAI, *ibid.*, ch. 26). Also the correspondence with the two algorithms discussed

14. See G. B. DANTZIG, 1963, chapter 23 for a short outline of the problem and its solution.
15. See J. KORNAI, 1967.

in this chapter will have made itself felt even now: one can conceive the *market* as the *central authority* assigning prices at each stage for all relevant items[16]. In the excess-demand method these prices are conveyed to buyers and suppliers at the markets, and an optimal programme is established from which the factor demands can be assessed. 'The market' observes a discrepancy, issues new prices, and so on. On the other hand, the excess-price method concentrates on prices[17], and also, only one side (either buyers or suppliers) of each market receives price instructions. The other side is left free to adjust its volume accordingly and reports the corresponding optimal price to the centre, and so on. The master programme in this case is formed by the required equality of demand and supply prices.

Owing to our preoccupation with the equilibrium aspects, the coverage of solution techniques for equilibrium programming problems has been intentionally one-sided. The purpose of discussing the two above algorithms was twofold. One objective was, of course, to present methods to solve such problems. But the other was to reveal more clearly the similarities between conditions for stability in the general equilibrium and conditions for convergence of a programming problem that derives its special character from a built-in equilibrium formulation. Other approaches which do not display this quality in such an explicit way, have so far been practically ignored. However, we have just seen that other procedures may possibly also be used.

Two-level planning can be interpreted to come very close to the excess-demand approach. But this only applies to a lesser degree for still *another procedure*, namely the algorithm presented by H. SCARF, 1969, based on the recent work of T. HANSEN, H. W. KUHN and H. SCARF. The property which places it apart from the algorithms discussed earlier in this chapter is that in this case no special requirements regarding demand and supply behaviour have to be fulfilled. It will not be necessary to underline that this feature renders the algorithm very attractive. Computationally, however, it is rather complex and elaborate.

In the first instance this algorithm adopts a bounded, but otherwise arbitrary set of price vectors of the dimension that corresponds with the problem to be solved. For each vector the activity with the highest positive profit is then determined. If such an activity exists, it is introduced as a counterpart to the price vector; if, however, all activities operate at

---

16. Indeed, S. A. MARGLIN, 1969, indicates how the Arrow-Hurwicz-Uzawa gradient method can be used to solve a central planning problem.
17. Recall, however, that one method is not the dual of the other.

a loss at this price set, the vector of corresponding demand volumes is introduced. Thus, one obtains an indication of demand and supply activities which are roughly in accordance with the adopted price region. Quite obviously there is no reason to expect the corresponding activities to produce exactly a feasible solution, but the algorithm provides a procedure which leads to feasibility in a finite number of steps in much the same fashion as the simplex algorithm does. The degree of precision of the final solution depends inversely on the size of the region enveloped by the price vectors, but the computation time increases of course when greater precision is required.

7. An illustrative equilibrium programming problem for Turkey

7.1. PURPOSE OF THE EXERCISE

The purpose of this exercise is to examine the working of a correction procedure on the basis of the excess-price approach in a *simple simulation* of the first stages of formulating a multi-sector plan. This type of simulation often proves to be useful, as it may point out some practical complications which are hard to foresee in a purely theoretical analysis or a numerical example. It will also illustrate more clearly the type of data needed and may finally clarify remaining obscurities.

The exercise does not pretend to end up with the outcome that would have been obtained if the price-consistency concept had been taken into proper account. One may even doubt if such a pretension can be maintained at all, but if it can, the exercise which must sustain it can hardly be a one-man job. The collection of data is a formidable task and requires the active participation of organizations like a statistical office or a planning bureau. In the present case parameters had sometimes to be borrowed from other countries than Turkey. So, even if the proportions and magnitudes are not unrealistic, for this reason alone, the exercise cannot claim to be authentic.

Also the refinements built into the basic model do not go beyond those of a simple type of multi-sector programming model. No distinction has been made, for example, between various skills, although the difference in scarcity would have justified such a breakdown. Since it would anyway have been impossible to carry out the exercise in a fully satisfactory way, a high degree of sophistication would have been of little use and could even have created unnecessary confusion.

The treatment of the price-consistency concept itself has been confined to the *price-equilibrium* aspect. It has been mentioned above that the price-realism aspect poses no new problems as far as the procedure itself is concerned. If only the structure of the model satisfies certain conditions so that the relevant dual prices can, in principle, attain positive values simultaneously[1], the only thing to be done is to insert some restrictions. In terms of the dual formulation, these restrictions can directly be imposed on the dual prices. This is the most direct attack. But the same effect can be achieved through a sensitivity analysis on the RHS terms of the corresponding constraints in the primal formulation. C.A. BLYTH and G.A. CROTHALL, 1965, present an illustration of the impact of a price restriction in a linear programming model for the New Zealand economy.

This exercise examines the price-equilibrium aspect exclusively in so far as the *foreign exchange rate* affects *export opportunities*. This is another serious limitation. Not so much because imports have been made independent of the exchange rate, since this assumption can reasonably be defended. More important is that many other items have been treated as if they were independent of prices, even though the price changes implicit in the solutions are often considerable. A notorious case is the relative composition of consumption which has, roughly speaking, been kept constant under significantly different commodity-price vectors.

For these reasons it will be clear that the exercise cannot claim even to come close to an acceptable treatment of the complications arising from the price-consistency problem. It also follows that no normative value can be attached for the Turkish economy to the final results of the exercise, even though the magnitudes are not unreasonable.

A detailed description of the main characteristics of the economy of Turkey has deliberately been omitted, since it would have created the impression that we are still concerned here with an actual application of an equilibrium-programming problem to Turkey. A number of these characteristics will indeed come up for discussion, but only in the course of the subsequent presentation when its progress requires it. Readers interested in more detailed information are referred to the publications[2].

The exercise relates to *1967*, the last year of the first five-year-plan period. Although it may seem a bit strange to choose a year in the past for a planning exercise, this arrangement has a few advantages. First, and most important, 1967 is the most recent year for which the State Planning Organization has drawn up a very detailed input-output table. Second, in that year the fact that the Turkish lira was seriously overvalued had made itself apparent in a number of ways, but devaluation had not yet taken place. Hence, in 1967 the external position was still in a state of disequilibrium. As the exercise is concerned with this very aspect, it is attractive to carry it out for such a year.

1. We come back to this below.
2. J.K. EASTHAM, 1964, A.O. KRUEGER, 1966, S. ILKIN and E. INANÇ, 1967, W.W. SNYDER, 1969, M.J. FRY, 1971, J. MCCABE and C. MICHALOPOULOS, 1971.

In order to play the game properly, we shall pretend to be placed in a year prior to 1967. It will appear that in that year we have already a pretty good idea of the structure of the economy in 1967, in terms of input and consumption coefficients, export opportunities etc. But there are still a few options open, so there is room for planning. The problem is now to examine the advantages of alternative activities and to select the best combination, while taking into particular account the need for price equilibrium in the foreign trade relations.

7.2. THE BASIC MODEL

A recurrent difficulty in more or less practical applications of multi-sector programming models arises from the *rigid structure* that most of these models possess. In mathematical programming problems there will evidently have to be possibilities to select between activities; in other words, the formulation of the problem must allow for degrees of freedom. But this is not only a question of counting variables and constraints. The opportunities for selection also depend on the composition of the model.

Starting from a determined multi-sector model, it is important to know whether a certain number of degrees of freedom have been created, by allowing for inequalities, or by allowing for choice between domestic production and imports, or between different production techniques. In the latter case selection opportunities are obviously much richer, since different activities with different *structures* are to be compared with each other, whereas the former case provides more freedom only in terms of activity *levels*.

On the other hand, if one unit of a certain activity in a linear model has been found to be attractive, any number of units of that activity will be so. This is because a *linear* evaluation system does not possess a mechanism which allows for different 'cost' and/or 'revenue' of one unit of an activity at different levels of operation.

For example, if in a linear multi-sector model the objective is to maximize consumption, only one type of consumption good will be produced, if no special precaution is taken. The product selected will then be the one that can be produced most cheaply and all available production factors will be used for this purpose. The outcome may be entirely unrealistic, but this is how the model exploits the freedom it has been allowed. The model has no more feeling for the possibilities in reality than has been put into it.

115

In practical exercises it will always be necessary to correct for the inherent bluntness of such models. It implies that the degrees of freedom which have been introduced at first, must be *reduced* considerably in the second instance in order to remain within a more or less realistic range of possible outcomes. But even then the model remains essentially linear, and the production functions are still of a complementary nature and do not allow for substitution between inputs. Subsequently it will be observed that there are cases where these aspects enforce further adaptations.

In the present model the opportunities for selection among alternative activities are the following:
i. the model allows for *import substitution* of *semi-finished products* by distinguishing two production activities for each type of output, where one activity obtains a greater portion of its intermediate goods from domestic production than the other;
ii. the possibility of *import substitution* also exists for some *finished products* (consumption and investment goods);
iii. a limited *choice* is possible among *consumer goods*.

It will appear that, notwithstanding the freedom thus created, the model is not yet sufficiently flexible for application of the price-realism aspect. This is not a serious limitation for our purpose, since we do not intend to incorporate this aspect in the exercise. It illustrates, however, the stringent demands that a full treatment of the price-consistency problem poses in terms of model formulation besides the data requirements.

We have now come to the algebraic presentation of the model[3]. It has been mentioned already that domestic production of every commodity category can be procured by two different activities:

$$(1-a_{ii}^1)x_i^1 - \Sigma a_{ij}^1 x_j^1 + (1-a_{ii}^2)x_i^2 - \Sigma a_{ij}^2 x_j^2 - c_i^p - j_i - e_i + m_i^c + m_i^j = c_i^q$$

$$(i = j = 1, ..., 13) \tag{7.1}$$

where a_{ij}^1 = input coefficient from sector i to sector j both of the first type of production activity;
x_i^1 = production of sector i of first type of production activity;
a_{ij}^2 = input coefficient from sector i to sector j both of the second type of production activity $(a_{ij}^2 \geq a_{ij}^1)$;
x_i^2 = production of sector i of second type of production activity;
c_i^p = private consumption of commodity i distinguished separately;

---

3. Exogenously determined variables appear as RHS terms.

116

j_i = investment of commodity i (excluding change in stocks) distinguished separately;

e_i = exports of product i;

m_i^c = 'variable' competitive imports of private consumer good i;

m_i^j = 'variable' competitive imports of investment good i;

c_i^g = public consumption of product i.

The model is left some freedom in terms of the *composition of private consumption*. That is to say, a minimum level of consumption amounting to ninety per cent of 'normal' consumption is required. But on top of that a margin of twenty per cent can be added, if attractive. It is for the model to decide which levels of consumption are thus to be enlarged.

In addition to this, import substitution is permitted up to twenty per cent of normal competitive imports, at the most. The remaining eighty per cent will be imported anyway and can, therefore, be treated in the same way as non-competitive imports. This can be expressed as follows (see also (7.9)):

$$c_i^p - 0.9 u_i y - \Delta c_i^p = 0 \tag{7.2}$$

$$\Delta c_i^p - 0.2 u_i y \le 0 \tag{7.3}$$

where u_i = 'normal', average propensity to consume commodity i produced domestically plus twenty per cent of the 'normal', average ratio of competitive imports of consumer good i to national income;

y = national income;

Δc_i^p = 'additional' consumption of commodity i.

The definition of total consumption is

$$c - n^c y - \Sigma c_i^p = \Sigma c_i^g \tag{7.4}$$

where c = total consumption;

n^c = proportion of non-competitive imports of private consumer goods plus eighty per cent of total competitive imports of private consumer goods to national income.

The composition of investments by products is strictly regulated by the investment relations, but import-substitution opportunities are arranged similarly. In this case only can import substitution reach up to forty per cent of normal competitive imports. Hence (see also (7.10)):

$$j_i - r_i j = 0 \tag{7.5}$$

$$j - \Sigma j_i - n^j j = 0 \qquad (\Sigma r_i + n^j = 1) \tag{7.6}$$

117

where r_i = proportion of domestically produced investment good i plus forty per cent of 'normal' competitive imports of investment good i in total investments;

j = gross investments (excluding changes in stocks);

n^j = proportion of non-competitive imports of investment goods plus sixty per cent of total competitive imports of investment goods in total investments.

In this case an additional constraint must be introduced regarding the *volume of investments*. The objective function of the model is to maximize consumption in 1967, so a strong tendency prevails to produce consumer goods at the expense of other final demand items. The next requirement can therefore be considered as a rather primitive terminal condition, which ensures that the productive capacity in the investment-goods industries is maintained at a normal level.

$$j - 0.15 y \geq 0 \tag{7.7}$$

The *export functions* will play a crucial role in a later part of the exercise where the price-equilibrium aspect will be incorporated, for these are the only functions which allow for *price dependency*.

$$e_i = e_i(\hat{z}) \tag{7.8}$$

where $\hat{z}$ = the foreign exchange rate under which the export opportunities are evaluated; the circumflex accent ($\hat{}$) indicates the in-price.

We have already mentioned that import substitution of consumer goods may reach twenty per cent of normal imports, but the opposite situation is also allowed by the model. By (7.9) namely, competitive imports of consumer goods can reach a maximum 1.2 times the normal level. It is composed of eighty per cent competitive imports treated as complementary imports (included in n^c in (7.4)), and an additional maximum of forty per cent in (7.9). However, if the additional competitive imports should settle at zero, a net import substitution of twenty per cent would result. A similar reasoning applies to the investment goods.

This formulation may seem unnecessarily elaborate, but saves in fact some additional constraints. It implies that m_i^c and m_i^j represent the *'variable'* part of the competitive imports of consumption and investment goods.

$$m_i^c - 0.4 v_i^c y \leq 0 \tag{7.9}$$

$$m_i^j - 0.8 v_i^j j \leq 0 \tag{7.10}$$

118

where v_i^c = 'normal' volume of competitive imports of private consumer
good i to national income;
v_i^j = 'normal' volume of competitive imports of investment good i
to total investment.

The *primary inputs* have been treated in the simplest possible way. In
an illustrative exercise as presented here, this is not very serious. But,
since the factors of production are among the most important items in
multi-sector models, they deserve very careful consideration in practical
applications. In this case all labour categories have been taken together,
without distinction between different skills or levels of training.

$$\Sigma l_j x_j^1 + \Sigma l_j x_j^2 \leq l \tag{7.11}$$

where l_j = labour-input coefficient of sector j;
l = labour force.

The next constraint represents the confrontation of capital supply with
capital use. The available capital stock in 1967 is supposed to be composed
of the capital stock of the previous year plus the investments produced in
the course of 1967. It has therefore been assumed that investments can
be used direct for production. In terms of model formulation a more
realistic treatment can be introduced rather easily, but for the present
purpose there is not much point in doing so.

$$\Sigma k_j x_j^1 + \Sigma k_j x_j^2 - j \leq \bar{k}_{-1} \tag{7.12}$$

where k_j = capital-input coefficient of sector j;
$\bar{k}_{-1}$ = capital stock in 1966.

The *balance-of-payments constraint*, again, is a very important one in
our analysis, since it generates the dual price of foreign exchange which
will be used in the algorithm for price equilibrium. To allow direct
comparison with the official exchange rate, this constraint has been
expressed in u.s. dollars. Subsequently, it will need special attention, but
at the present stage there are no complications. Note that the import
requirements of the second type of production activity are smaller – if
there is a difference – than those of the first type. This is because the
former type of activity has a greater preference for domestic inputs than
the other type.

$$\frac{1}{2}(\Sigma m_j^1 x_j^1 + \Sigma m_j^2 x_j^2 + n^c y + n^j j + \Sigma m_i^c + \Sigma m_i^j - \Sigma e_i) \leq \bar{d} \tag{7.13}[4]$$

4. This expression will subsequently be modified (see section 7.5).

119

where m_j^1 = import coefficient of sector j of first type of production activity;

m_j^2 = import coefficient of sector j of second type of production activity $(m_j^2 \leq m_j^1; \sum_i a_{ij}^1 + m_j^1 = \sum_i a_{ij}^2 + m_j^2)$;

$\bar{d}$ = maximum permissible deficit on the balance of trade in U.S. dollars.

The *national income definition* now follows easily. It reads:

$$y - c - j - \Sigma e_i + m = 0 \tag{7.14}$$

where m = total imports (sum of positive elements between brackets in (7.13)).

The *objective* of the model is the maximization of total consumption, but, since public consumption has been fixed exogenously, only private consumption is actually maximized. In fact, this is a slight deviation from the aims of the Turkish plan, which do not include the maximization of consumption. Since growth of GNP obtains a high priority, it would perhaps have seemed more natural to optimize national product rather than consumption. This has not been done, because dual prices are somewhat easier to interpret if they relate to consumption outlays. In any case, given the structure of the model, the optimization of national product and of consumption do not conflict; on the contrary, they tend to run parallel. Moreover, future growth of GNP has been secured by the minimum-investment requirement. So:

maximize c. $\tag{7.15}$

If the constraints and unknown variables were now counted, one would overestimate the actual size of the problem considerably, for a fairly large number of variables would operate only at zero level[5]. These variables and the corresponding constraints can therefore be omitted without consequence for the outcome of the model. Hence, 13 constraints remain in (7.1), 12 in (7.2) and (7.3), 5 in (7.5), 11 in (7.8), 8 in (7.9) and 2 in (7.10). Further, some equations can be substituted without much inconvenience. In principle, of course, all equations can be substituted, but such an operation would reduce the comprehensibility of the model. This observation is important for the interpretation of the findings, so it must be taken into consideration with the required computer time, if an efficient dimension of the problem is to be determined.

5. The next section indicates which variables are involved.

In the present case only equations (7.2) and (7.5) have been eliminated. This very cautious policy has been prompted by the fact that the model is to be used ultimately for an exercise with which little experience is available. Thus, the problem consists altogether of 53 constraints and 88 unknown variables, including 26 slack variables.

7.3. PRESENTATION OF THE PARAMETERS

The data required for the above model have been taken as much as possible from material provided in the 1967 input-output table and a study entitled *Third Five Year Development Plan, growth model and its solutions*, both prepared by the long term planning section of the Turkish State Planning Organization. The input-output table is very detailed in the sense that it distinguishes for 37 sectors between three components

Table 7.1. A description of thirteen aggregated sectors

Code and name of aggregated sectors	Name and code of original sectors
1. Agriculture	Agriculture (1), Forestry (2), Animal husbandry and fishing (3)
2. Mining	Coal mining (4), Iron ore mining (5), Other mining and quarrying (6)
3. Food processing	Sugar refining (7), Tobacco prods. (8), Alcoholic beverages (9), Other food processing ind. (10)
4. Light industries	Textiles and apparel (11), Wood prods. (12), Leather prods. (14), Rubber and plastic prods. (15)
5. Chemicals	Paper and printing (13), Chemicals and pharmaceuticals (16), Fertilizers (17), Petroleum and coal prods. (18)
6. Building materials	Non-metallic mineral prods. (19), Cement (20)
7. Iron and steel	Iron and steel ind. (21), Non-ferrous metal ind. (22), Metal prods. (23)
8. Machinery	Machinery (24), Electrical machinery (25), Transport equipment (26)
9. Electricity	Electricity (27), Public services (36)
10. Transportation	Railway transportation (28), Other transportation (29), Communications (31)
11. Trade	Trade (30), Banking, insurance etc. (32), Professions (33)
12. Construction	Building construction (34), Non-building construction (35)
13. Ownership of dwellings	Ownership of dwellings (37)

Table 7.2. Domestic input coefficients, competitive import coefficients (both taken from Turkish I-O table, 1967) and complementary import coefficients (see text)

Sectors	1	2	3	4	5	6	7	8	9	10	11	12	13
1*	.22132	.02991	.40389	.14287	.00718	.00159	0	0	0	.00466	.01847	.01340	.0
	.00006	0	.00168	.01074	.00345	0	0	0	0	0	0	0	0
2	.0	.00712	.00432	.00240	.05234	.08390	.02256	.01766	.01341	.00566	.00240	.02050	.00894
	.00002	0	0	0	0	0	.00033	0	0	0	0	.00026	0
3*	.01463	.0	.09332	.00097	.10566	.00159	.00016	.02172	0	.03349	.02168	0	0
	.00002	.0	.00157	.00578	.00842	0	0	.01258	0	.00122	.00023	0	0
4*	.00238	.00189	.02474	.12995	.00911	.00902	.00300	.01725	.00970	.09132	.02187	.04722	0
	.00060	.0	.00056	.01262	.00538	0	.00217	.00345	.00038	.00641	.00061	.00026	0
5*	.01078	.02611	.00813	.00616	.00414	.06585	.07820	.00040	.01940	.00145	.01173	.03417	.00811
	.00543	.00474	.00101	.03013	.05745	.00743	.00534	.00446	.00171	0	.00169	.00113	0
6*	.0	.00237	.00347	.00120	.05773	.03345	.00668	.02030	.00028	.00198	.00235	.08455	.00395
	.0	.0	.0	.00060	.00220	.02124	.00200	0	0	.00005	.00028	.00788	0
7	.00121	.01709	.01391	.00668	.02679	.01911	.22125	.12893	.00998	.05304	.00650	.11206	.00103
	.00011	.00142	.0	.00225	.00013	0	.06734	.04670	.00085	0	.00065	.01209	0
8	.00386	.02136	.00207	.00225	.00276	.02336	.01888	.16527	.00447	.00151	.00155	.02611	0
	.00002	.0	.0	.00067	.00345	0	.00066	.02030	0	0	.00004	.00026	0
9	.00112	.02754	.00757	.01563	.00262	.05469	.03225	.01786	.01255	.00910	.01074	.00122	.00124
	.0	.0	.0	.0	.01118	0	0	0	0	0	0	0	0
10	.01112	.02896	.04164	.03074	.03093	.03823	.05681	.01908	.00332	.10119	.02337	.04538	.00395
	.0	.0	.0	.0	0	0	0	0	0	0	0	0	0
11	.02350	.04748	.05224	.06779	.05732	.10568	.04879	.05279	.03462	0	.06151	.10505	.03306
	.0	.0	.0	.0	0	0	0	0	.00028	0	.00113	0	0
12	.0	.0	.0	.0	.0	.0	.0	.0	.0	.0	0	0	0
	.0	.0	.0	.0	.0	.0	.0	.0	.0	.0	0	0	0
13	.0	.0	.0	.0	.0	.0	.0	.0	.0	.0	.06184	0	0
	.0	.0	.0	.0	.0	.0	.0	.0	.0	.0	0	0	0
Complementary import coefficients	.04568	.03322	.05628	.06425	.02030	.03080	.04250	.03319	.00180	.04408	.04348	.00771	.0

of inputs, namely domestic inputs, competitive imports and tax on competitive imports. Final demand is broken down into the following items: public and private consumption, investments, changes in stocks, exports and competitive imports. Non-competitive imports have been treated as complementary inputs. This information has been used for the calculation of the parameters in the above model. But in order to keep the model within manageable proportions, the table has been *aggregated to thirteen sectors*. Table 7.1 describes the newly obtained sectors in terms of the original sectors.

The input coefficients have been presented in table 7.2. Each cell contains two elements; the upper element indicates domestic inputs and the lower element relates to inputs of competitive imports. These data have been used to establish two matrices of input coefficients, A^1 and A^2 respectively. Matrix A^1 contains only the domestic input coefficients. They are identical with the coefficients a_{ij}^1 of the previous section, and the corresponding vector of import coefficients (the m_j^1) consists of the complementary import coefficients plus the sum of the competitive import coefficients by columns.

Matrix A^2 allows for import substitution by adding fifty per cent of the competitive imports to the domestic input coefficients, but only in the rows which have been indicated by an asterisk in table 7.2. The remaining competitive imports have been added in the same fashion to the complementary import coefficients, to obtain the vector of the m_j^2.

Without a correction, this set-up would have allowed for considerably more import substitution than is actually attainable in 1967. Therefore, the complementary import coefficients have been raised somewhat so that the import substitution resulted in import levels *around* the actual import volumes, and *not* consistently *below* the latter.

The parameters given in table 7.3 require only little comment. The first four columns present coefficients which have been derived from the input-output table. The capital-output ratios, however, have been taken from the growth model for the Third Five Year Plan period, although they have been defined there as incremental capital-output ratios. They are, therefore, of an approximate nature, also because they refer to the period 1973–1977.

Since the labour coefficients, as needed here, are not available for Turkey, they have been taken from a different country, in this case South Korea[6]. There is no reason to assume that these figures are better appli-

6. See Economic Planning Board, 1965, p. 126 and p. 127 for manufacturing and mining industries and p. 197 for remaining sectors.

cable than the coefficients of another country in the same income bracket. In the present problem they do not affect the outcomes, because in each solution the labour constraint proves not to be binding. On the other hand, if the price-realism aspect had been taken into account by requiring that the dual wage equated the market wage, the situation would have been entirely different. The labour constraint would have been forced to become effective then, so that the magnitude of the labour coefficients would have influenced the outcome.

Table 7.3. Other coefficients and constant terms used in the model

	u_i (1)	r_i (2)	v_i^c (3)	v_i^j (4)	l_j (5)	k_j (6)	c_i^g (7)	e_i if $\hat{p}_f = 9$ (8)
				Coefficients				Constant (RHS) terms (in million TL)
1	.21804				235.923	1.90187	102	3310
2	.00232				45.881	3.17099	42	150
3	.13977				7.473	0.54999	750	400
4	.08399		.00075		16.127	0.73745	335	80
5	.02199		.00303		10.683	0.91643	229	30
6	.00514		.00013		17.745	0.99118	14	10
7	.00724	.01569	.00099	.01625	12.483	1.52731	270	150
8	.01178	.10281	.00397	.11610	11.904	0.59528	164	10
9	.00834		.00256		33.059	3.79260	8233	220
10	.13107	.01139	.00307		34.327	1.76097	350	550
11	.11256	.02937	.00419		75.668	0.50404	397	800
12		.65990			25.131	0.23400		
13	.03686				23.644	11.49000		

$n^c = 0.00323 + 0.8 \times 0.01869 = 0.01818$
$n^j = 0.10142 + 0.6 \times 0.13235 = 0.18083$

Finally, the public consumption and export figures have been taken direct from the 1967 input-output table. Instead of these actual observations we could also have taken the planned performances as given in the First Five Year Plan. Although the outcome of the exercise might have been different, the procedure which is most important here, would, of course, be unaffected. The main reason why the actual figures have been used is that the plan does not specify the exports it foresees for all the sectors distinguished here.

Although some of the figures 'plugged into' the model refer to the actual performances, recall that we are pretending to carry out the exercise in a year before 1967. Hence, the export volumes, for example, should be regarded as accurate estimates of the export opportunities in 1967, assuming that the foreign exchange rate will then still be nine TL to the dollar (the official rate in that year).

The only RHS terms which have not yet been evaluated are now l, $\bar{k}_{-1}$ and $\bar{d}$. The first symbol stands for the available stock of labour. This variable is rather difficult to measure accurately, but this is not very serious for the present problem. From experience we know that the manpower population rarely deviates much from a level of forty per cent of total population. Thus, the Turkish population in 1967 being nearly 35 million, the magnitude of l has been put at 14 million.

A direct estimate of the capital stock is even more difficult to obtain. Here the capital stock in 1966 plus investments during 1967 to the amount of fifteen per cent of national income have been required to be large enough to allow a growth rate of GNP during 1967 of seven per cent (the growth target in the Turkish plan). Applying the weighted average of the sectoral capital-output ratios in column (6) of table 7.3, the required value of $\bar{k}_{-1}$ is found to be 250,000 million TL.

The maximum permissible deficit on the balance of trade has been fixed at $900 million. This corresponds roughly with the actual deficit according to the 1967 input-output table when the official exchange rate is applied. Observe that $\bar{d}$ does not represent the current account deficit. The latter is considerably smaller owing to transfers of Turkish workers abroad.

7.4. THE NAIVE SOLUTION

Although both the formulation of the model and some of its parameters deviate somewhat from the 1967 input-output structure, the resemblance is, however, sufficiently strong to cause a high degree of similarity also between the solution of the model and the magnitudes in the input-output table. The values of some of the key variables have been given in table 7.4, where s_l (the slack variable in the labour constraint) indicates the level of unemployment.

But these values are not of great importance. It is much more interesting to examine how the model has used the freedom it has been permitted, for this gives an indication of the scarcities – and, therefore, the bottle-necks – in the economy according to the model. If the model has some realistic significance, this information can be very helpful when preparing the formulation of an economic policy.

Table 7.4. Actual and computed value of some key variables (rounded off to nearest hundred)

	y (in mln TL)	c (in mln TL)	j (in mln TL)	s_l
Actual value	90,400[a]	86,500	17,300	...
Solution value	93,600	87,500	14,000	34,000

a. Excl. change in stocks.

Looking at the solution values in this way, it becomes immediately clear that the three prime factors distinguished in the model display *different scarcity* patterns under the market price prevailing in 1967. *Foreign exchange* is the scarcest factor of production. This follows from the observation that the solution has used every opportunity to economize on foreign exchange. Imports of final demand items have been reduced to a minimum level, or, which is the same, import substitution has been pushed to its maximum. Also import substitution of intermediate products has been fully exploited, for only production activities of the second type appear in the optimal basis. Finally, the sectors selected for production of 'additional consumption' (the Δc_i) are clearly those which use relatively small amounts of foreign exchange. They are the sectors 1, 4, 6, 9, 10 and 11, all of the second type of production activity.

Import substitution economizes on foreign exchange, but it requires more *capital*. The fact that the optimal solution chooses overwhelmingly for import substitution and against imports provides an indication that it has found foreign exchange to be more scarce than capital. Still, the capital constraint is binding, so capital is a scarce factor in this solution.

As one would expect, *labour* comes last, being the least scarce factor of the three. In fact, it is not really scarce at all, since a part of the available manpower remains unused. Of course, the model does *not predict* a level of unemployment of 34,000 people. The solution states that even if (i) labour costs are zero, *but* if (ii) the relevant parameters were *perfectly price inelastic* (to be unaffected by a drop in wages from their actual 1967 level to zero), 34,000 people would remain jobless. In reality labour costs will not be zero, so employment opportunities will be even smaller than the solution indicates.

126

The limited importance of solutions to linear programming problems as this one for practical purposes has been emphasized in earlier parts of the text. But the above discussion has shown that they can still provide some valuable information. For when one examines the choice made between two or more alternatives, one finds an indication of the tight sections of the economy (which the solution avoids). This is also precisely the way in which the solutions are used in the excess-price algorithm.

On the other hand, the absolute levels at which the variables operate in this solution are of little interest, because they prove to be *unattainable*. The dual solution shows that the prices of the crucial prime factors adopted for evaluation of the activities in the model are:

i.   foreign exchange rate $(p_f) = 32.3$ TL/\$;
ii. interest rate $(p_k) = 16.7$ per cent;
iii. wage level $(p_l) = 0$.

Two of these prices deviate vastly from the actual market prices; only the rate of interest is probably not very unrealistic. Consequently, the outcome of an evaluation on the basis of such a different price set cannot claim practical significance.

Hence, even if the parameters of the model and the constraints in which they appear give an accurate and complete description of the Turkish economy, and if the objective function and the constraints were to represent the targets of the Turkish plan adequately, the above consideration renders pointless any attempt to achieve the magnitudes indicated by the solution. The reason, as we know, is that the price system stands in the way of achievement, and it would be senseless to go for it all the same. If it is nevertheless used for this purpose, we get a *naive solution*.

In order to be able to cope with the price inconsistencies which characterize the naive solution one must know the flexibility of the prices of the commodities and primary factors in the model. The price-equilibrium aspect which arises when prices are flexible will be the main subject of discussion in the next two sections. So let us concentrate in the rest of this section on the consequences for the model if prices lack flexibility, that is, when the price-realism aspect has to be taken into account.

In principle, the introduction of *price constraints* does not create serious difficulties. If we take the price of labour as an example, two ways seem to be open. One way to force the dual wage rate upwards is to reduce the labour supply. This can be continued until the dual wage rate has reached a level which corresponds approximately with the market wage. Obviously the 'labour supply' which brings about this equality of dual and market wage must now be interpreted as *employed labour*. For now it indicates the number of workers *actually* employed when the solution values would apply, since the labour-demand pattern – as indicated by the labour-input coefficients – is in accordance with the dual wage.

An alternative approach is to formulate the problem in its dual form, in order to introduce the price restriction direct. In the Turkish case the dual wage could be required to be not less than, say, 5,000 or 6,000 TL. A further consideration expressed in section 4.5. must now also be reiterated. In the preceding paragraph it was indicated how the market wage can be effectuated by lowering the RHS term in the primal labour constraint. So in the corresponding dual formulation one *cannot* insist on maintaining the *same* magnitude either. The simplest solution is to treat l in (7.11) as an endogenous variable in the primal form and to add a separate constraint which puts an upper limit on l equal to the original labour supply. Thereafter the problem can be dualized. In the dual solution to this dual problem the value of l will then represent employed labour just as in the other approach.

Real difficulties would only come up when the price-realism aspect is to be tackled with the aid of a model which is not sufficiently equipped to this end. The model we are now dealing with belongs to this category. The problem is that the model can generate practically only two non-zero prices of prime factors simultaneously. Such an outcome would be perfectly acceptable, if it correctly represented a structural phenomenon characteristic for the economy described in the model. But this is not the case; the property just mentioned is akin to the *structure of the model*, and in this way it does not do justice to the real world, where the phenomenon does not exist. The problem is that the elbow-room lent by the model is its present formulation is just sufficient to accomodate two prime factors in the basis. If the third factor is forced into the basis in one of the ways indicated above, room can be created for it only by the departure of one of the two factors that were in already. This is not satisfactory, for even though it may be realistic that one or more factors operate with a slack activity, it is not acceptable that a position where all factors have positive prices is ruled out entirely.

In order to repair this defect we must first know more about its cause. In fact, it was mentioned at the beginning of section 7.2. when the rigidity of linear multi-sector models was briefly introduced. Two factors were indicated as being mainly responsible for this: the linearity of the constraints, and the limited variety of choice between alternative activities.

The selection procedure in the simplex algorithm economizes on inputs which are very scarce and, therefore, expensive, whilst using as much as possible of the inputs which are cheap. So if an input is not fully used in the optimal solution, this is because the feasible area did not reach far enough. For example, rather ample substitution opportunities have been built into the model between foreign exchange on the one hand, and domestic inputs (labour and capital) on the other. Thus we have seen that these have all been exploited when the algorithm found foreign exchange to be particularly scarce and consequently shifted as far as possible towards the use of domestic inputs.

However, such substitution opportunities among labour and capital have hardly been permitted and have in fact been limited to the *indirect* substitution possibilities involved by the selection between 'additional' consumer goods. But here too the scarcity of foreign exchange dominated, that is sectors using relatively little foreign currency had priority over sectors using much labour and relatively little capital, so that the indirect substitution among the domestic inputs had only little effect. Hence, the obvious solution to our problem is to introduce activities which offer *direct* substitution possibilities of labour for capital, and inversely. Most effective is a differentiation between labour-intensive and labour-extensive technologies. If adopted, this approach would have raised the number of types of production activities to three.

It has been said in subsection 2.2.2. that the actual substitution possibilities appear to be limited. So when a variety of production techniques is proposed here, this must be accompanied by a warning against exaggeration. Still, in reality some degree of substitution is possible and the input coefficients obtained from an input-output table represent in fact a weighted average of the different techniques. It is therefore perfectly acceptable to allow for alternative input structures, if only they remain within a reasonable distance from the average observed.

In a practical application the problem will, again, be to obtain the necessary information for a sufficiently accurate description of the alternative techniques. But since the exercise does not include the price-realism aspect, this complication need not bother us now.

7.5. THE PROBLEM OF CONSTANT PRICES

One of the purposes of the exercise was to find out about possible practical complications in an application of an equilibrium programming algorithm which may otherwise be overlooked. Perhaps the problem of constant prices is such a complication.

The problem is the following. In each iteration of any algorithm towards price equilibrium a different price set is used to evaluate the parameters in the problem. Also the final price vector which corresponds with the equilibrium will be different from the prices in which the problem was expressed originally. It is very inconvenient, however, if all these changing price vectors are also used in *value expressions*.

Suppose indeed that the values of the relevant items in a programming problem are expressed by variable prices. Obviously a comparison of different outcomes would thus be complicated tremendously. In our exercise we should have difficulty in comparing the solution values with the actual magnitudes in 1967. But this is not even very serious, since only two sets of values are to be compared. For, in order to be useful for policy formulation, a considerably larger number of runs must be made with a mathematical model to scan sensitivities and alternatives. These outcomes must, of course, be comparable one with another. So if different price expressions should hamper, or even prevent this, special precautions must be taken.

Briefly: a comparison of two different values for one and the same item is facilitated considerably, if the difference is a real difference. This occurs if the items are expressed in constant prices. For the application of the algorithms this implies that a distinction must be made between the prices employed to evaluate the parameters in physical units and the prices used in value expressions, where only the former are allowed to vary. The actual algorithm is of course in no way influenced by this complication. In practice it means that for each model to which an equilibrium programming algorithm is applied, we must determine separately how constant prices can be maintained in value expressions. This operation requires great care. But as soon as the necessary corrections have been established, their application becomes a routine operation.

As an illustration let us consider how these considerations affect the exercise. The price dependency which sets off the application of the excess-price algorithm in the next section is confined to the influence of a changing foreign exchange in-price on export opportunities. So when we want to maintain constant prices we only have to be concerned with this price.

The effect of a simulated devaluation on export volumes can take different forms. First we examine the case when the *domestic price* remains *constant*, and when the benefit of the price decrease in foreign currency is passed on to the foreign buyer of the export goods. The competitive position of the exporting country on the world market will thereby be improved and the result will be an increase in the export quantities. Precisely this increase interests us, because we want the change resulting from evaluation on the basis of a different exchange rate to be expressed in real terms. The extent of the increase depends of course on the relevant price elasticities.

So, if upper indices *1* and *2* indicate here the situation before and after devaluation respectively, q_i stands for the export quantity of product *i*, s_i for the price elasticity of exporting product *i*, and p_f for the foreign exchange rate, we obtain

case 1; domestic export prices constant $$q_i^2 = q_i^1 + \frac{p_f^1 - p_f^2}{p_f^2} s_i q_i^1 \qquad (7.16)$$

Since domestic export prices in this case are constant – as we want them to be in value expressions – the new export values to be substituted in the model can be found after multiplying e_i^1 by $\left(\frac{p_f^1 - p_f^2}{p_f^2} s_i + 1 \right)$.

Unfortunately, the foreign exchange revenue does not increase proportionally with the export quantities, because the export price in foreign currency has gone down. More quantity units must now be exported than before devaluation in order to earn the same amount of foreign currency. Only if elasticity is smaller than minus one will the foreign exchange earnings increase, but only because the quantity increment more than offsets the price reduction. In *real terms*, however, the foreign exchange earning capacity of exports has *dropped* by the same rate as the devaluation. And since the commodity-balance constraint (7.13) is expressed in dollars, this implies that in this case the export variables in that constraint must be divided by the *new* exchange rate.

The second case describes the situation where the export price expressed in foreign currency does not change, so there is no inducement for foreign buyers to import more from the devaluing country than they would have done without the devaluation. But, in terms of domestic currency, exporters get more value for each quantity unit they sell. This price increase we want to eliminate, so we ignore it in the expression of domestic export values. Since the quantity component does not change either, this implies that

case 2; foreign export prices constant $$e_i^2 = e_i^1 \qquad (7.17)$$

If the new exchange rate were also applied in this case to translate these unchanged export values into the dollar values in which (7.13) has been expressed, the latter values would decrease. This would be incorrect, so the *original* exchange rate must be used here.

131

The impression that this case does not provide opportunities for improving a devaluing country's external position must be avoided, however. The domestic revenue increase will stimulate producers of international goods to sell a greater part of their output to abroad. Producers who did not even consider exportation previously may find it sufficiently attractive after a devaluation. The extent of this *export-promotion effect on the supply side* depends of course on the elasticity of supply of international goods and on the success of exporters in finding new buyers abroad.

Very little is known empirically about this effect which is often over-looked anyway. For countries with a reasonably diversified production structure its impact may still be considerable. But then eq. (7.17) does not hold any longer and must be replaced by an equation which indicates the extent of the gain in exports. The advantage here is of course that the foreign-exchange earning capacity is not affected.

One does not expect to find corresponding cases regarding the treatment of imports, for, as a general rule, the price of import goods expressed in foreign currency will remain constant after devaluation. Therefore, domestic import prices will rise. This is where the similarity with the above-mentioned case 2 ends, because this time demand is on the domestic end and it is likely to be affected by the rise of import prices in terms of domestic currency. Together with the constant foreign prices, a decrease of imports in quantity units implies a reduction of demand for foreign currency.

This change in imports in physical terms is precisely what we want to capture in the new parameters, but no more than that. The extent of the change depends of course on the relevant import price-elasticities. But since the prices in the value expressions of the model do not change, the original exchange rate must be maintained in the balance-of-trade constraint to translate the domestic import value into foreign currency.

According to this reasoning it may seem as if the beneficial influence exerted by a devaluation has a better chance with imports than with exports. Any decrease in physical imports reduces the pressure on the foreign currency position, whilst only those export items with a price elasticity of foreign demand greater than one (in absolute terms) will have the same effect. In reality, however, the situation is somewhat different.

Before a devaluation actually takes place, excess demand for foreign exchange has in most cases existed for some time. The pressure which has thus been building up is often kept under control by quantitative restrictions on imports which put the official price mechanism out of action. As a consequence, the effect of a devaluation on physical imports will be very much diluted, for it will first have to wipe out the excess demand before it can cut into the existing import volumes.

In 1967 Turkish imports were characterized by an extremely tight regulation system. Under these conditions a devaluation can hardly be expected to have much influence on the physical quantities of imports. This is why all parameters describing the structure of imports in the model are unaffected by the different foreign exchange in-prices which are adopted in the various steps of the algorithm. Only export volumes have been made dependent on the exchange rate.

7.6. RESULTS OF THE ITERATIVE PROCEDURE TOWARDS CONVERGENCE

The practical complication arising from the need to maintain constant prices in applications of equilibrium programming algorithms has just been related. The excess-price algorithm which has been applied in this exercise has already been presented and illustrated in earlier parts of the text. So we can now confine ourselves to a description of the assumptions regarding the export behaviour in the model and a brief discussion of the results of the exercise.

Table 7.5. Assumed price elasticities of foreign demand for the export products in the model

Sector code	Sector description[a]	Export values in 1967 in millions of TL	Assumed price elasticities
1	Agriculture	3310	
2	Mining	150	−1.2
3	Food processing	400	−1.1
4	Light industries	80	−2.5
5	Chemicals	30	−2.0
6	Building materials	10	−1.0
7	Iron and steel	150	−1.2
8	Machinery	10	−1.2
9	Electricity	220	
10	Transportation	550	−1.5
11	Trade	800	−1.8

a. For a more detailed sector description, see table 7.1.

133

The *price elasticities* which have been assumed to represent the reaction of the quantities exported to a change in the price of foreign exchange have been tabulated above. The values of these parameters have been fixed more or less arbitrarily and there is no particular reason why they should hold for the demand behaviour of Turkey's export products. However, information on the price elasticities of the Turkish export products which we have distinguished in the model is not available. The relative values of the elasticities given in the table are a mixture of the author's subjective judgement of Turkey's export opportunities and the relative composition of price elasticities actually observed for similar commodity categories in different (mainly industrialized) countries[7]. The absolute magnitudes will be discussed subsequently.

The export commodities have been broken down into *two groups* corresponding with cases 1 and 2 of the previous section. Case 1 applies to the commodities which become cheaper in foreign currency after devaluation and which can, therefore, be sold in larger volumes to countries abroad. For this group we need indeed the price elasticities of foreign demand.

The other group, however, to which case 2 applies, consists of commodities which have been assumed not to be affected by the devaluation, because their foreign prices remain unchanged. Agricultural products have been included in this category, because their prices are often bound by regulations and agreements. The price formation of electricity and public services is often governed by considerations which place them apart from other products or services. It has been assumed, rather arbitrarily, that this is reflected in a constant price in terms of dollars.

The other commodity groups have all been treated under case 1. This is of course too simple a picture to be acceptable for practical purposes. In reality, very probably, the characteristic reaction of exports to a devaluation will lie *in between* the two cases considered here. A rise in domestic export prices will thus be accompanied by a decrease in the foreign price, in such a way that the price advantage created by a devaluation is shared by the domestic suppliers and the foreign buyers of the export products. In that case the export-promotion effect resulting from higher profitability of exports must also be taken into account. This effect has not been included in the exercise, even though it is likely to be very

7. For a survey of publications on price elasticities in foreign trade, see B. BALASSA, 1967. Sources are, for example, B.A. DE VRIES, 1951, R.J. BALL and K. MARWAH, 1962, R.R. RHOMBERG and L. BOISSONNEAULT, 1964, R.M. STERN, 1964, J.M. MCGEEHAN, 1968 and H.S. HOUTHAKKER and S.P. MAGEE, 1969.

important for a country like Turkey, where industrialization is already well under way.

A minor complication arises from the fact that all export products have not been treated in the same fashion. As we know, exports of products 1 and 9 and all imports must be divided by the original exchange rate of nine TL per $ in the balance-of-trade constraint. The other export products, however, must be divided by the particular in-price of foreign exchange which changes with each step. As a result, the external deficit in TL is different for each step of the algorithm, even though it remains constant in terms of dollars.

The foreign exchange earnings of sectors 1 and 9 are unaffected by a devaluation. Further, the export price-elasticities of the goods and services produced by the other sectors are smaller than, or at least equal to minus one. As a result the export earnings in foreign currency can only increase in the event of a devaluation, and since import outlays have been made constant, *a rise in the price of foreign exchange* will *reduce the deficit* on the balance of trade. Inversely a reduction of the rate of exchange will bring about a larger deficit.

If the relation between exchange rate and external deficit were different, neither the excess-demand[8] nor the excess-price algorithm would converge. In this way the model complies with the requirement that substitution effects in a price-dependence relation must 'dominate' for convergence. For this exercise it implies that exports measured in dollars must rise if the exchange rate goes up. (Compare with (6.51). The sign is different there, because the expression relates do demand items.)

Finally, we come to *the outcomes of the iteration process*. It was mentioned already that the naive solution comes up with a dual price of foreign currency of 32.3 TL per U.S. dollar. This result is obtained with the actually observed export volumes in the model which hold under the official exchange rate of 9 TL to the dollar. It suggests that this rate undervalues foreign currency, so in the next iteration of the excess-price algorithm a price higher than the official rate, but lower than the dual price is to be used to evaluate export opportunities. In fact, the adaptation made in each iteration has been fixed at an arbitrary sixty per cent of the difference between in and out-price.

The table and the graph which now follow, describe the adaptation

---

8. According to eq. (6.21), which describes the export behaviour in the Chenery-Uzawa model, it may seem that only a negative price elasticity of foreign demand is required in the excess-demand algorithm. However, this requirement is subsequently strengthened by (6.32). Indeed, in the illustrative example which goes with that model only price elasticities smaller than minus one have been employed.

path followed by the algorithm towards the point of convergence, or perhaps it is better to speak of *the point next to convergence*. We observe – and this is illustrated clearly by graph 7.1. – that the adaptation process in the very final stage is stuck between two adjacent solutions, neither of which is exactly an equilibrium solution.

Table 7.6. In and out-prices of foreign exchange through the iterations

Iteration	In-price in TL per $	Out-price in TL per $	Difference
1 (naive solution)	9	32.34	+23.34
2	23	12.49	−10.51
3	17	12.49	−4.51
4	14	12.49	−1.51
5	13	15.55	+2.55
6	13.50	15.55	+2.05
7	13.75	15.55	+1.80
8	13.85	12.49	−1.36

But this is much less serious than it may seem at first sight. It is caused by the fact that the relation between in and out-prices is discontinuous, because a change in the dual prices in the exercise can arise only from a change of the optimal basis. So if the algorithm steers towards a price which is *between* the dual prices corresponding with two neighbouring optimal solutions, it will continue to hesitate between these two points. In that case it *cannot* indicate *exactly* the equilibrium values of the variables in the model. However, since the model cannot pretend anyway to represent the real world exactly, such an outcome still provides very useful information, if only the two solutions are not too far apart. For practical purposes it is of course sufficient to know the values of the variables in the nearest to equilibrium solutions which have been located. There is no practical reason to insist on still more precise information.

The first indication that the algorithm does not settle down at one equilibrium solution can be obtained after step 5. During the earlier steps the algorithm seems to proceed rapidly to the convergence point. After the fifth iteration it is clear that an in-price lower than 13 will direct the next step upwards, whereas an in-price higher than 14 will point downwards. So one expects to find the equilibrium price somewhere between 13 and 14 TL per dollar.

136

It is also evident that the adaptation after step 5 should be less than sixty per cent of the difference between in and out-price. Otherwise we return into an area which has been explored already, whereas it is more interesting to scan the range of in-prices between 13 and 14 TL per dollar. This is done in steps 6, 7 and 8; we find that the change of basis takes place near a foreign exchange in-price of approximately 13.80 TL to the dollar.

The relation between in and out-prices as calculated in the iterations is indicated clearly by graph 7.1. The interrupted line connecting the points observed in steps 1 and 5 is an approximation of the 'kinked' curve which actually connects these two points, but which has not been calculated.

Graph 7.1. The relation between in and out-prices (the figures indicate the steps in the algorithm)

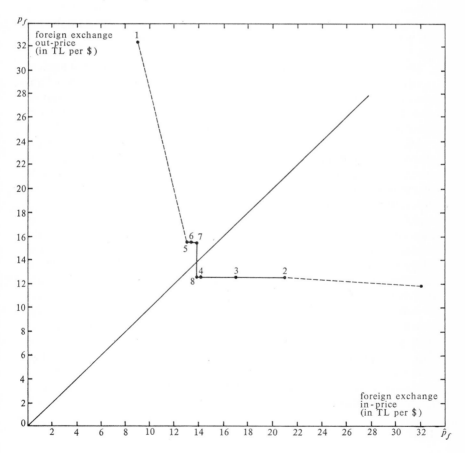

The 45° line through the origin indicates the potential equilibrium points, since on this line in-prices are exactly equal to out-prices. If it intersects a *horizontal* section of the curve, we have a *precise* equilibrium point. We have an *approximation* of the equilibrium, if it intersects a *vertical* section, as it does in the present case. The point $(\hat{p}_f, p_f) = (32.0, 11.8)$ does not play a role in the algorithm. It has only been calculated to enhance the artistic appeal of the graph.

It has been emphasized above that the exercise as carried out here is unfit to be used for planning purposes. The shortcomings have already been discussed; obviously they affect the usefulness of the outcome. The gravest deficiency is probably the fact that the model permits a wage level of zero, whereas in reality total wages constitute the major share in national income. Also this has been mentioned before, but it may be necessary to reiterate these points again in order to underline that the outcomes of this exercise – partly presented in table 7.7 – do not possess a normative value. Therefore, it is a coincidence that the equilibrium margin found in the exercise indeed includes the new exchange rate after the 1970 devaluation of fifteen TL per dollar.

The exercise has illustrated the rather impressive amount of statistical information which is required for an equilibrium programming problem, even if it is still too primitive to be practically useful. It has also shown that the model to be used in order to tackle the price-consistency problem satisfactorily should be built with particularly great care.

More concretely, the outcome of the simulation has demonstrated, amongst other things, that a simple approach which does not account for price inconsistencies can create a distorted view of the desirable levels of the relevant magnitudes in a development process. It is true that the differences between the solution values in column (2) of table 7.7 on the one hand, and those in columns (3) and (4) on the other, are not very impressive. But this is, of course, because the correction for price inconsistencies in the exercise has been limited to the exchange rate only. Moreover, it has been assumed that alterations in the exchange rate do not affect the largest export item (agricultural products) which is probably not realistic. Further, the Turkish economy being rather closed, changes in external trade do not influence other magnitudes very considerably. But if we concentrate on the exchange rate itself, we notice that the first dual price *overestimates* the 'equilibrium rate' by a very large degree. This corresponds with an earlier suspicion (see section 4.4.). The difference between the first in-price and its dual counterpart is larger still. It means, of course, that the solution values obtained in the first instance cannot be realized. For this reason it would be incorrect to conclude from table 7.7

138

Table 7.7. A selection of actual and solution values

Symbols and units of measurement	Actual values (1)	Step 1 (naive solution) ($\hat{p}_f = 9$) (2)	Step 7 ($\hat{p}_f = 13.75$) (3)	Step 8 ($p_f = 13.85$) (4)
primal solution				
y (in mlns TL)	90,376[a]	93,589	94,464	94,490
c (in mlns TL)	86,466	87,535	86,959	86,928
j (in mlns TL)	17,295	14,038	14,170	14,173
s_l (unemployment)	...	33,979	676,045	687,117
e_1 (in mlns $)	368	368	368	368
e_2 (in mlns $)	17	17	18	18
e_3 (in mlns $)	44	44	46	46
e_4 (in mlns $)	9	9	14	14
e_5 (in mlns $)	3	3	4	5
e_6 (in mlns $)	1	1	1	1
e_7 (in mlns $)	17	17	18	18
e_8 (in mlns $)	1	1	1	1
e_9 (in mlns $)	24	24	24	24
e_{10} (in mlns $)	61	61	72	72
e_{11} (in mlns $)	89	89	113	114
Δc_1 (in mlns TL)	...	4,081	0	0
Δc_3 (in mlns TL)	...	0	1,194	1,059
Δc_4 (in mlns TL)	...	381	1,576	1,576
Δc_5 (in mlns TL)	...	0	416	416
Δc_6 (in mlns TL)	...	96	97	97
Δc_8 (in mlns TL)	...	0	126	223
Δc_9 (in mlns TL)	...	89	0	0
Δc_{10} (in mlns TL)	...	2,453	2,476	2,476
Δc_{11} (in mlns TL)	...	2,107	2,126	2,127
m_9^c (in mlns TL)	1	0	0	1
dual solution				
p_f in TL/$	9	32.34	15.55	12.49
p_k in %	...	16.70	28.40	30.60
p_l	...	0.0	0.0	0.0

a. Excludes change in stocks for comparability with solution values.

that consumption goes down if the price-equilibrium aspect is taken into consideration, since the naive solution values just do not hold.

8. Summary and conclusions

8.1. SUMMARY[1]

In any comprehensive development planning procedure there is one stage in which a confrontation takes place of demand for and supply of factors of production and commodities or commodity categories. The objective is, of course, to see to it that the plan does not require more of the necessary items than can actually be made available.

Indeed, the technique which is commonly used for that purpose (input-output analysis) does just that. The price system is not considered, however, even though the prices under which supply and demand will match deserve, of course, special attention here. In this connection, it is often argued that, in combination with another technique (linear programming), one can also obtain an impression of the scarcity ratios of the relevant factors and products, if the requirements involved by the plan are to be met.

But there is a serious problem here. Planning always refers to a future period, and direct observations are ruled out. Actual observations relate to the actual situation which is partly determined by the prevailing prices (market prices). This actually prevailing socio-economic structure is practically always the point of departure for a development plan.

In a linear programming model this structure is represented by the parameters which, as was just remarked, are a reflection of the actual prices, amongst other things. But the scarcity ratios (*dual prices*) obtained from a linear programming application are determined precisely by the parameters, and therefore also by the *market prices*. In other words, the dual prices are themselves dependent on the set of prices behind the parameters in the model. If the dual prices are used to determine the parameters the latter are likely to change, so that in the second instance

---

1. Brief summaries have already been inserted in preceding parts of the text. So the reader may find it useful to glance at sections 1.1. and 4.6. as well.

again *different* dual prices would be derived from the model. It follows that dual prices *are not necessarily equilibrium prices*.

The solution to a linear programming problem assumes that the corresponding dual prices hold. Nevertheless, they are often vastly different from the actual, market prices, and, in any case, they cannot hold as long as they are not equilibrium prices. As a consequence, the confrontation of supply and demand will almost certainly lead to an inconsistency, if a corrective procedure is not applied. Without it, however, the plan would be wrong.

Such an inconsistency has been called here a price inconsistency. It leads to two questions:

i. can a technique be provided which is capable of indicating both the *equilibrium volumes* of factors and products to be exchanged according to the plan, as well as the *equilibrium prices* involved?

ii. how must one cope with *actual prices* which can *vary* only *between narrow bounds*, so that the equilibrium prices become irrelevant?

These two questions indicate the subject matter of this book. It must be emphasized, however, that the price-inconsistency problem is not confined to applications of mathematical programming. Any development plan involves a certain scarcity pattern, independent of the question whether it has been formulated on an intuitive basis, or using a different approach, such as, for example, linear programming. Therefore, price inconsistencies are equally likely in all planning procedures which do not correct for them.

The only difference is that in applications of linear programming, the corresponding scarcity patterns are made explicit by the dual prices, whereas they remain obscure in other approaches. So, for reasons of both exposition and analysis, this technique is particularly attractive when treating the subject of this book.

The price-consistency problem would not arise, if the market prices underlying the plan were equilibrium prices. It is well-known, however, that the prices of primary factors in developing countries are very much in *disequilibrium*. These are also precisely the prices with the greatest impact on the rest of the economy, which explains the practical importance of this problem.

These disequilibria are caused by different circumstances. For example, for very good reasons the wage rate cannot drop below a certain minimum. But this curtails demand for labour and explains partly the massive unemployment rates in many less developed countries. The rate of interest is often kept artificially low in order to stimulate investment, with an excess demand for capital as a probable outcome. Also the exchange rate often underestimates the scarcity of foreign currency partly for the same reason, and with a similar result.

The market is less than a reliable guide towards socio-economic development in poor countries. Hence, *price intervention* may be fully justified, but it is necessary to take into account also the possible mis-allocation it entails. On the other hand, if a price remains *fixed* at a certain level, the plan should take this fact into account (chapter 2).

A rigid market price can be turned into a lower effective price by subsidies. Such a procedure could, for example, be considered for the wage rate, if the equilibrium wage is lower than the actual minimum-wage level. Unfortunately, there are *administrative* and/or *financial* complications which may even be so severe that they practically rule out its application. The problem is aggravated by the amount of the transfers involved which tends to be very considerable indeed. Again, if these complications cannot reasonably be solved, the plan must be made consistent with the *price restrictions* (chapter 3).

In the practice of development planning, the price system has received only very little attention so far. We have seen that this is likely to result in an inconsistency which is not only of theoretical interest, but which may easily have important practical consequences. In order to cope with the problem an additional effort must be made, first, because new data are required, and, second, because a corrective procedure must be applied using this new information. Fortunately, the *price-realism aspect* (relating to question (ii) above) creates only relatively little trouble. Moreover, in those cases where this aspect applies because the relevant market price is fixed, the *price-equilibrium aspect* (relating to question (i) above) does not arise. The latter aspect poses great demands in terms of statistical information (price elasticities) and solution procedure (chapter 4).

The price-equilibrium theory must provide the theoretical background for solving the price-equilibrium aspect. Two adaptation patterns – simulating the adaptation behaviour in a situation of price disequilibrium towards the new equilibrium – have been examined in some detail; they are the excess-demand and the excess-price pattern. Ever larger market systems have been considered – involving increasingly wide interdependences, until a set-up was reached coinciding with the breakdown into products and primary factors commonly adopted in the type of confrontations as mentioned in the opening paragraph of this chapter.

The conditions to be fulfilled in order that a price equilibrium be reached deserve special attention. Not surprisingly, the essential conditions regarding the market behaviour of suppliers and buyers prove to be basically the same in simple and more extensive market structures. Their reasonability in a general sense is not in doubt. The usefulness of the theory for practical purposes becomes questionable, however, due to the bold, *simplifying assumptions* which have to be made in the most comprehensive case dealt with here in order to keep the problem within manageable proportions (chapter 5).

The mathematical programming problem which emerges when the price-equilibrium requirement is imposed on a linear programming problem is not a non-linear programming problem as we know it. This new problem might be called a *general-equilibrium programming problem*. Two algorithms by which it can be tackled have been discussed and compared. They are derived from the excess-demand and excess-price adaptation patterns respectively, and strong *similarities* exist between the conditions for attaining a stable equilibrium on the one hand, and those for convergence of the algorithms on the other. The correspondence with two-level planning is also remarkable. This procedure is one among other available algorithms which have been briefly indicated and which can also be considered for solving the price-equilibrium problem (chapter 6).

The illustrative exercise for Turkey serves as a *simulation* of the application of the excess-price algorithm. It also helps to demonstrate in more concrete terms the requirements which a multi-sector model must satisfy in order in theory to deal with the price-realism and the price-equilibrium aspect. In fact rather wide opportunities for substitution among primary factors must be built into the model.

A practical complication is caused by the fact that prices in a price-equilibrium problem are variable. On the other hand, in order to facilitate comparison of actual values and solution values, or among values in different solutions, it is necessary to employ *constant prices*. Hence, the (variable) prices used in evaluations in the model must be distinguished from the (constant) prices used in value expressions.

The exercise further demonstrates that the algorithm may end up in a situation where it is unable to decide between *two adjacent solutions*, neither of which is precisely the optimum-equilibrium solution. This is because dual prices in a sensitivity analysis on RHS terms jump abruptly from one value to another. So if the equilibrium price lies in the discontinuous interval, the two cannot equate and the algorithm can only provide an approximation of the equilibrium. For practical purposes this is not at all serious, if only the approximation is not too crude. Finally, taking into acount the limitations of the exercise, it is clearly illustrated that the *difference* between equilibrium and naive solution can be considerable (chapter 7).

8.2. GENERAL CONCLUSIONS

In this book we have been confronted with a practical complication arising in development planning procedures. The obvious question now is whether we can expect to be able to deal with it. I think the answer is uncertain and cannot be given in one word.

We have observed already that analysis of the price-equilibrium aspect requires an impressive amount of *additional information*. Moreover, any of the solution procedures discussed more or less extensively in chapter 6 requires an additional effort and a technical skill which will be available only in relatively few developing countries.

Each of these circumstances may prove to be an insuperable obstacle to the application of a correction procedure for many countries. But let us assume for a few moments that these complications do not exist, or can be surmounted, in order to see what lies beyond them.

Thus we come to the workability of the *solution procedure* itself. After what has been said about the *weakness of the theoretical basis* in chapter 5 and taking into account the inevitable simplifications that a simulation of reality involves (chapter 7), it is clear that one cannot be entirely confident. On the other hand, the practical workability is not disproved by these deficiencies.

Kornai states that 'only those theorems and propositions (deduced from assumptions not in conflict with reality) which describe the real world more or less accurately may be considered acceptable'[2]. He concludes after a comprehensive analysis that the general equilibrium theory *cannot meet this requirement*. The tentative conclusion derived from our much more modest excursion into this theory agrees with Kornai's. Still, the correction procedures may prove to be workable propositions. This depends on the distortions resulting from the simplifying assumptions underlying the algorithms, and the extent to which these affect the correspondence with reality. In the absence of practical experience this question remains unsettled.

An analysis which would examine for a variety of countries whether or not the deviations of actual development from the development foreseen by a price-inconsistent plan can be explained by the neglect for the price consistency, would be very useful. For the sake of simplicity such an analysis should preferably exclude those countries for which the deviations can clearly be attributed to other causes. The exercise would have to render explicit the scarcity ratios involved by the plan (in terms of,

2. J. KORNAI, 1971, p. 9.

for example, dual prices) and confront them with the corresponding prices which prevailed in reality. If there is a difference, the effect if the actual prices are imposed upon the plan should be examined[3]. Some constraints must then be left free, of course, but otherwise the basic characteristics of the plan should be left intact as far as possible.

Even if the observed deviations and the simulated deviations found in an exercise as described were to agree, this would not show that the correction procedure for the price-equilibrium aspect would work, for that is a different matter. But one would then at least be able to foresee and specify the error caused by price inconsistency. Still, it would probably also increase one's confidence in the excess-price correction towards price equilibrium, for it is based on information regarding scarcity ratios.

Subsequent to his negative evaluation of the general equilibrium theory, Kornai advocates *a different approach* and defines some areas of research which should be investigated to this end. Indeed, there is much to be said for this attitude when one looks at the still feeble structure of the present theory and compares it with the very impressive efforts which have been put into it. Certainly it is worth while under these circumstances to start anew in an attempt to build a theory that is more powerful for analytical and planning purposes than the present one.

Still, it would be mere speculation if we were to indicate at this stage which of the two will ultimately be the best[4]. Even if the present theory is in an unsatisfactory state, the necessary breakthrough may still come. On the other hand, economic science and its applications can only gain if an alternative theory were to challenge successfully the present theory or an extension of it. In the meantime operational procedures which are meant to cope with practical problems must find their origin in the available theory in whose realm the problem resides. The criterion by which such procedures should be judged until a better one is proposed, is the contribution which, if applied, they make towards the solution of the problem.

3. In a price-consistent planning procedure, this situation would also arise, if, for price realism, all market prices have to be pre-fixed, because they cannot change in the real world.
4. See also L. Johansen's review of Kornai's book (L. JOHANSEN, 1970).

References

ALLEN, R.G.D. (1964), *Basic mathematics*, Macmillan & Co. Ltd., London.

ARROW, K.J. (1959), Toward a theory of price adjustment, in ABRAMOVITZ, M. *et al.*, *The allocation of economic resources*, Stanford University Press, Stanford.

ARROW, K.J. and HAHN, F.H. (1971), *General competitive analysis*, Holden-Day, San Francisco, Oliver & Boyd, Edinburgh.

ARROW, K.J., HURWICZ, L. and UZAWA, H. (eds.) (1958), *Studies in linear and non-linear programming*, Stanford University Press, Stanford.

BACHA, E. and TAYLOR, L. (1971), Foreign exchange shadow prices: a critical review of current theories, *The Quarterly Review of Economics*, vol. 85, no. 2.

BALASSA, B. (1967), *Trade liberalization among industrial countries, objectives and alternatives*, McGraw-Hill Book Company, New York.

BALL, R.J. and MARWAH, K. (1962), The U.S. demand for imports 1948-1958, *The Review of Economics and Statistics*, vol. 44, no. 4.

BAUER, P.T. and YAMEY, B.S. (1963), *The economics of under-developed countries*, James Nisbet and Cy Ltd. and Cambridge University Press, Digswell Place (5th printing).

BLYTH, C.A. and CROTHALL, G.A. (1965), A pilot programming model of New Zealand economic development, *Econometrica*, vol. 23, no. 2.

BRUNO, M. (1967), The optimal selection of export-promoting and import-substituting projects, in United Nations, *Planning the External Sector: Techniques, Problems and Policies*, report on the First Interregional Seminar on Development Planning, New York.

CAGAN, P.D. (1956), The monetary dynamics of hyperinflation, in FRIEDMAN, M. (ed.), *Studies in the quantity theory of money*, University of Chicago, Chicago.

CHAKRAVARTY, S. (1964), The use of shadow prices in programme evaluation, in ROSENSTEIN-RODAN, P.N. (ed.), *Capital formation and economic development*, MIT Press, Cambridge (Mass.).

CHANDAVARKAR, A.G. (1970), Interest rate policies in developing countries, *Finance and Development*, vol. 7. no. 1.

CHENERY, H.B. (1955), The role of industrialization in development programs, *American Economic Review*, vol. 45, no. 2.

CHENERY, H.B. (1959), Interdependence of investment decisions, in ABRAMOVITZ, M. *et al.*, *The allocation of economic resources*, Stanford University Press, Stanford.

CHENERY, H.B. and KRETSCHMER, K.S. (1956), Resource allocation for economic development, *Econometrica*, vol. 24, no. 4.

146

CHENERY, H. B. and UZAWA, H. (1958), Non-linear programming in economic development, in ARROW, K. J., HURWICZ, L. and UZAWA, H. (eds.), *Studies in linear and non-linear programming*, Stanford University Press, Stanford.

CHENERY, H. B. and WATANABE, T. (1958), International comparison of the structure of production, *Econometrica*, vol. 26, no. 4.

CHIANG, A. C. (1967), *Fundamental methods of mathematical economics*, McGraw-Hill Book Company, Inc., New York.

CORNELISSE, P. A. and VERSLUIS, J. (1969), The semi-input-output method under upper bounds, in BOS, H. C. (ed.), *Towards balanced international growth*, North-Holland Publishing Company, Amsterdam.

DANTZIG, G. B. (1963), *Linear programming and extensions*, Princeton University Press, Princeton.

DEBREU, G. (1959), *Theory of value, and axiomatic analysis of economic equilibrium*, Monograph 17 of the Cowles Foundation, John Wiley & Sons, Inc., New York.

DORFMAN, R. (1964), *The price system*, Prentice-Hall, Inc., Englewood Cliffs (N.J.).

EASTHAM, J. K. (1964), The Turkish development plan: The first five years, *Economic Journal*, vol. 74, March 1964.

ECKSTEIN, P. (1968), *Accounting prices as a tool of development planning*, Center for Research on Economic Development, University of Michigan, Michigan.

FRY, M. J. (1971), Turkey's first five-year development plan, an assessment, *Economic Journal*, vol. 81, June 1971.

HADLEY, G. (1964), *Nonlinear and dynamic programming*, Addison-Wesley Publishing Company, Inc., Reading (Mass.).

HANSEN, B. (1970), *A survey of general equilibrium systems*, McGraw-Hill Book Company, Inc., New York.

HICKS, J. R. (1946), *Value and capital*, Oxford University Press, London (2nd edition).

HOUTHAKKER, H. S. and MAGEE, S. P. (1969), Income and price elasticities in world demand, *The Review of Economics and Statistics*, vol. 51, no. 2.

ILKIN, S. and INANÇ, E. (eds.) (1967), *Planning in Turkey*, Middle East Technical University, Ankara.

JOHANSEN, L. (1970), Book review of J. Kornai's anti-equilibrium, *Economics of Planning*, vol. 10, no. 3.

Korean Economic Planning Board (1965), *Korea statistical yearbook*.

KORNAI, J. (1967), *Mathematical planning of structural decisions*, North-Holland Publishing Company, Amsterdam.

KORNAI, J. (1971), *Anti-equilibrium*, North-Holland Publishing Company, Amsterdam.

KOYCK, L. M. (1954), *Distributed lags and investment analysis*, North-Holland Publishing Company, Amsterdam.

KRUEGER, A. O. (1966), Some economic costs of exchange control: the Turkish case, *Journal of Political Economy*, vol. 74, October 1966.

KUENNE, R. E. (1963), *The theory of general economic equilibrium*, Princeton University Press, Princeton.

147

LANGE, O. and TAYLOR, F. M. (LIPPINCOTT, B. J., ed.) (1938), *On the economic theory of socialism*, The University of Minnesota Press, Minneapolis.

LEFTWICH, R. H. (1966), *The price system and resource allocation*, Holt, Rinehart and Winston, New York (3rd edition).

LEWIS, J. P. (1972), *The public-works approach to low-end poverty problems: the new potentialities of an old answer*, paper presented to the Committee for Development Planning, United Nations ECOSOC.

LITTLE, I. M. D. (1963), *A critique of welfare economics*, Oxford University Press, London (2nd edition).

LITTLE, I. M. D. and MIRRLEES, J. A. (1969), *Manual of industrial project analysis*, vol. II: *Social cost benefit analysis*, Organisation for Economic Co-operation and Development, Paris.

MACHLUP, F. (1958), Equilibrium and disequilibrium: misplaced concreteness and disguised politics, in *Economic Journal*, vol. 68, March 1958, reprinted in MACHLUP, F. (1963), *Essays on economic semantics*, Prentice-Hall, Inc., Englewood Cliffs (N.J.).

MARGLIN, S. A. (1969), Information in price and command systems of planning, in MARGOLIS, J. and GUITTON, H. (eds.), *Public economics*, Macmillan, London.

MARSDEN, K. (1970), Progressive technologies for developing countries, in *International Labour Review*, vol. 101, no. 5.

MCCABE, J. and MICHALOPOULOS, C. (1971), *Investment composition and employment in Turkey*, AID discussion paper nr. 22, AID, Washington.

MCGEEHAN, J. M. (1968), Competitiveness: a survey of recent literature, *Economic Journal*, vol. 78, June 1968.

MENNES, L. B. M., TINBERGEN, J. and WAARDENBURG, J. G. (1969), *The element of space in development planning*, North-Holland Publishing Company, Amsterdam.

MIRACLE, M. P. and FETTER, B. (1970), Backward-sloping labor-supply functions and African economic behavior, in *Economic Development and Change*, vol. 18, no. 2.

MORISHIMA, M. (1964), *Equilibrium, stability and growth*, Oxford University Press, London.

MOUSTACCHI, M. (1965), *Application d'un modèle d'allocation des ressources à la planification française – ses enseignements*, paper presented at the World Econometric Congress, Rome.

MYRDAL, G. (1968), *Asian drama, an inquiry into the poverty of nations*, Pantheon, New York.

NEGISHI, T. (1962), The stability of a competitive economy: a survey article, in *Econometrica*, vol. 30, no. 4.

NOWZAD, B. (1969), Economic integration in Central and West Africa, *IMF Staff Papers*, vol. 16, no. 1.

NURKSE, R. (1961), *Problems of capital formation in underdeveloped countries*, Oxford University Press, New York.

QAYUM, A. (1960), *Theory and policy of accounting prices*, North-Holland Publishing Company, Amsterdam.

RHOMBERG, R. R. and BOISSONNEAULT, L. (1964), Effects of income and price changes on the U.S. balance of payments, *IMF Staff Papers*, vol. 11, no. 1.

SAMUELSON, P. A. (1947, 1965), *Foundations of economic analysis*, Harvard University Press, Cambridge (Mass.), and Atheneum, New York.

SCARF, H. (1969), *An example of an algorithm for calculating general equilibrium prices*, Cowles Foundation discussion paper no. 276, Cowles Foundation at Yale University New Haven (Conn.).

SCHREUEL, E.J. (1970), *Some empirical aspects of the incremental capital-output ratio*, paper no. 6, Centre for Development Planning of the Netherlands School of Economics, Rotterdam.

SCITOVSKY, T. (1951), *Welfare and competition, the economics of a fully employed economy*, Richard D. Irwin, Inc., Homewood (Ill.).

SIMON, G. (1970), Trends and stability of economy-wide prices, in CARTER, A.P. and BRÓDY, A. (eds.), *Contributions to input-output analysis*, volume I, North-Holland Publishing Company, Amsterdam.

SIMPSON, D. and TSUKUI, J. (1965), The fundamental structure of input-output tables, an international comparison, *The Review of Economics and Statistics*, vol. 47, no. 4.

SNYDER, W.W. (1969), Turkish economic development: the first five year plan, 1963–67, in *The Journal of Development Studies*, vol. 6, no. 1.

SOLIGO, R. (1971), Real and illusory aspects of an overvalued exchange rate: the Pakistan case, in *Oxford Economic Papers*, vol. 23, no. 1.

STERN, R.M. (1964), The U.S. tariff and the efficiency of the U.S. economy, *American Economic Review*, vol. 54, no. 2.

STOLPER, W.F. (1966), *Planning without facts, lessons in resource allocation from Nigeria's development*, Harvard University Press, Cambridge (Mass.).

TINBERGEN, J. (1956), *Economic policy: principles and design*, North-Holland Publishing Company, Amsterdam.

TINBERGEN, J. (1958), *The design of development*, The Johns Hopkins Press, Baltimore.

TINBERGEN, J. (1965), International, national, regional and local industries, in CAVES, R.E., JOHNSON, H.G. and KENEN, P.B. (eds.), *Trade, growth and the balance of payments*, North-Holland Publishing Company, Amsterdam.

TINBERGEN, J. (1967), *Development planning*, World University Library, London.

TODARO, M.P. (1969), A theoretical note on labour as an 'inferior' factor in less developed countries, *The Journal of Development Studies*, vol. 5, no. 4.

Turkish State Planning Organization (1972), *Third five year development plan, growth model and its solutions*, Ankara.

UZAWA, H. (1958), Iterative methods for concave programming, in ARROW, K.J., HURWICZ, L. and UZAWA, H. (eds.), *Studies in linear and non-linear programming*, Stanford University Press, Stanford.

VRIES, B.A. DE (1951), Price elasticities of demand for individual commodities imported into the United States, *IMF Staff Papers*, vol. 1, April 1951.

WALLIS, K.F. (1969), Some recent developments in applied econometrics: dynamic models and simultaneous equation systems, *The Journal of Economic Literature*, vol. 7, no. 3.

WINSTON, G.C. (1970), *Corruption and industrial growth under artificial exchange rates*, research memorandum no. 38 of the Center for Development Economics, Williams College, Williamstown (Mass.).

Indices

151

152